empty. S P A C E:
Where is My Stuff?

Soror DeRamus—
Thankyou for your
worthy example! I
hope you enjoy the
book.

Space—
Knight

empty. S P A C E: Where is My Stuff?

Navigating the Quarterlife Crisis with Wisdom and Skill

Kenya Jackson, MS

**_BOOK_**LOGIX®

Alpharetta, Georgia

ISBN: 978-1-61005-318-1
Library of Congress Control Number: 2013903199

Printed in the United States of America

∞This paper meets the requirements of ANSI/NISO Z39.48-1992 (Permanence of Paper)

Disclaimer: This book and the contents therein are offered as advice, and for guidance only. The author accepts no liability for the consequences of any actions, negligent or otherwise, based on the information provided. If financial, legal, or other expert help is required, the services of a qualified professional should be sought.

Front and back cover photo by Kareem Quow of KQ Photography
Special Thanks to Crystal Williams and Alex Howard for the use of their home to shoot the front and back cover.

Dedicated to -

Ms. Iyanla Vanzant for introducing me to the
concept of self-help writing.
Also, for Mr. Eckhart Tolle
and the five-letter word that changed my life,

SPACE.

The **Quarterlife Crisis** is the period of questioning and self-doubt that accompanies the transition into adulthood.

It most notably affects young adults, beginning in the early twenties.

Contents

Acknowledgments

To my partner, Michelle—
thank you for your patience.

To my aunt Aleese, and my cousin Kecia—
thank you for your support and wisdom.

To my mother, the late Gwendolyn Jackson—
thank you for your sacrifice.

For every disappointment and painful experience—
thank you for the gift of contrast.

"Just as no sound can exist without silence, nothing can exist without no-thing, without the empty space that enables it to be."

–Eckhart Tolle

INTRODUCTION:
Where is My Stuff?

25 years old
three degrees
unemployed
single
$100,000 in debt

That was my reality five years ago, when I started writing this book.

I was in the emotional choke-hold of a quarterlife crisis and I was pissed off!

I had spent twenty years in school and had absolutely nothing to show for it.

I thought to myself, how could I have made all the right choices and still have nothing but a ton of debt, no means to pay it back, and this permeating feeling of failure? What is more, like other young people who have gone through a similar experience, I felt cheated. I wondered where all the things were that I was promised as a child?

In a fit of anger and desperation, I posed one hypothetical question to the Universe. Where–is–my-stuff? Finding the answer to this question led me on a five-year spiritual journey; and in the midst of it, I discovered empty. S P A C E.

A play on words, representing both the physical empty space of not having something and the infinite potential encompassed in the Universe, *empty. S P A C E: Where is my Stuff? Navigating the Quarterlife Crisis with Wisdom and Skill* picks up where other books on the subject leave off. It does so by illustrating how a healthy relationship with the "empty no-thingness" of the Universe can help assuage feelings of failure and insecurity both during the quarterlife crisis and in later years.

In being the emptiness, empty. S P A C E holds the potential for any and every thing. Throughout the book, this term is used as a synonym for opportunity.

What it is–What it Ain't

WARNING: This is not one of those cheesy, cheerleader-y, "you can do it" self-help books. This is not the type of book that attempts to lump all the problems of the quarterlife crisis into three arbitrary (and socially constructed categories) like finance, relationships, and health. I won't be giving you ten or twelve steps to financial freedom. I won't be listing and quoting a bunch of hoity-toity, happy-go-lucky millionaires who have no problems because they paid them all to go away. I also won't be dusting off any old spiritual texts and telling you to "let go and let God." This book is not about things, steps, clichés or surrendering your power to a distant superhero in the sky.

This book is about real life. It's about a real person, who had a real crisis. It's about someone who learned to use her thoughts as allies instead of enemies, and that even in the emptiness there is value, and most importantly, potential. This book, and the stories within it, is not a manual—it's a tool.

Since our thoughts are the jumping-off point for all that we experience, it only seems fitting to start our little "stuff excavation" by discussing what we think and how we think about it. That conversation starts with one three-letter word that has four-letter implications.

E-G-O. Ego.

Ego and empty. S P A C E

Ego is defined by both Webster and Sigmund Freud as one of three mental constructs forming the structural basis for how we think. The other two parts of this trilogy are the *id* and the *super-ego*. The id is defined as the pleasure principle. It's the part of our minds that is purely impulsive. All it wants to do is get its needs met. It doesn't care about social norms or proper etiquette. It wants what it wants, and it doesn't care how it has to get it. Early psychologists likened the id to an infant child.

The super-ego, on the other hand, works in contradiction to the id. The super-ego strives to act in a socially appropriate manner. It strives for perfection and controls our sense of right and wrong with emotions like guilt and fear. You could imagine the super-ego like an overbearing parent.

Smack dab in the middle of these two is ego. The ego is charged with keeping order between them. Put simply, it provides the balance between what you want to do and what you think you should do. Because of this, the ego is constantly evaluating and reevaluating your impulses vs. your inhibitions. This causes a great deal of anxiety. In an effort to quell this anxiety, the ego develops an insidious need to know, possess, and evaluate things and ideas. It becomes the consummate judge.

Ego defines; it guides. It is a natural functional part of our minds. As a result, losing the ego will not provide the peace that so many others have claimed it will. Learning to manage the ego is the goal.

Let me back up for a moment though, because I want to do a little conceptual autopsy on the ego. The ego has some help in seeking to rationalize the demands of the id with the requirements of the super-ego. I have named the ego's allies **Tools of the Ego** or **TotEs**. In my study, I have extracted four TotEs: attachment, judgment, fear and destruction. I came up with these tools based on my experience, the experiences of those around me, and through my continued study of modern metaphysics[1]. In the pages that follow, each tool will be discussed in detail. In the meantime, we can imagine the Tools of the Ego as branches on the ego's tree. Each tool is mutually exclusive, so their impact is great whether any or all of them is present.

As human beings, we are uniquely crafted to encompass that which is purely logical or purely functional, while simultaneously possessing the ability to operate in the purely mystical. The mystical part of us can be defined as spirit, or empty. S P A C E. The word **empty. S P A C E** represents the cosmic emptiness that gives birth to all form and all life. The idea behind highlighting this emptiness is to show that in nothingness, anything and everything is possible.

---

[1] Metaphysics is the study or examination of the true nature of reality.

That being said, let's take a moment to notice how ego and empty. S P A C E work together in perfect unison on a daily basis.

Naturally, there has to be an equally powerful and functional **Tool of the Spirit** to accompany each Tool of the Ego. The Tools of the Spirit are not quick fixes; they are simply thinking strategies that can be used to gently usher you toward mental balance. The Tools of the Spirit are: appreciation, compassion, enthusiasm, and creation.

Each of the chapters that follow will discuss a Tool of the Ego as it relates to its corresponding Tool of the Spirit. I have found that it's in the juxtaposition of these tools that we find our ever elusive…stuff.

The book is organized into three parts. The first two parts focus on the relationship between the Tools of the Ego and the Tools of the Spirit. The final section is composed of blog entries. The blog entries detail the process of self-actualization that I underwent while grappling with the Tools of the Ego during my quarterlife crisis.

Section summaries are included below.

Crisis of Thought and Action

The quarterlife crisis is a crisis of thought and action orchestrated by the ego and its tools. Each of these tools builds upon the others to create the thoughts and subsequent experiences that we call crisis, failure, and so on. I have organized this book to reflect the natural way in which each Tool of the Ego both relates to and builds upon the others.

Part 1 – Crisis of Thought: Attachment and Judgment

Since attachment is the mechanism by which we identify and define ourselves, and judgment is the mechanism by which we identify and define other people, we must first experience attachment and judgment in order for every other Tool of the Ego to exist. As such, attachment and judgment are root Tools of the Ego. They are crises of thought—meaning that every other Tool of the Ego discussed in this book was first a function of attachment by way of identification.

Part 2 – Crisis of Action: Fear and Destruction

Fear is a manifestation of the accumulated attachments and judgments that we have deemed unpleasant or unwanted. It prevents us from thinking and behaving in ways that are not in alignment with previously accepted attachments and judgments. Indirectly, our inability to move outside of our comfort zone causes us to become destructive. We destroy the possibility of all that we could be by clinging so closely to all that we have decided or been told to be.

Release your attachments and the judgment will also cease. Without judgment, there will be no basis for fear. In the absence of fear you will no longer feel the need to be destructive.

Come into alignment with all that you really are. Your true self. The you that existed before your name, before your gender, and before your religious or political affiliations. These are mere ideas. Choices- carrying only as much weight and relevance as you assign them. Your body is a myth. Your ideas are arbitrary. Understand that you are the physical embodiment of source energy; that which gives birth to all form but is completely without form. You are the epitome of empty. S P A C E.

At the end of the day, when the sun meets the moon, all we have is our mind. Our mind is the key to creation. Our mind is what fills the emptiness with the stuff (things, people, and experiences) that we want.

Part 3 – Reflections on Crisis: This is my real life!

I hand-wrote this book on the floor of my apartment in the summer of 2008. At first, the chapters were just thoughts, random scribblings that I etched on individual sheets of notebook paper. More than just journal entries or stories, the chapters I wrote were subject based. I'd write a topic on the top the paper and just unload for hours at time. One day, I gathered all the papers together and put them in a white three ring binder. With silver stickers I wrote the word "S P A C E" in an arc across the front of the binder. The idea to make the contents of that binder a book didn't come until two years later.

As such, a lot of what you will see in this book came from journal entries and personal reflections. I've chosen to include some of these writings not only because they speak to this book's origin, but also because they embody the truth of both my quarterlife crisis and my transition out of it.

A "Right Alignment"

Danger is in extremes, not occurrences alone. So in the spirit of symmetry, let's decide not to think of the ego as an enemy. Instead, let's choose to think of our lives as a see-saw with ego on the left side of that see-saw. Much like the psychological components of the left brain, the ego is responsible for expressing analytic thought and logic.

On the other side of the see-saw is empty. S P A C E, or spirit. The right side is where we find holistic thought, intuition, and creativity. In the middle, perfect balance. Our choices are responsible for tilting the see-saw one way or the other. This book and metaphysics proper are designed to help us make more informed choices; choices that lead to balance and harmony. However, a large portion of the world is completely unconscious as to how much their choices can influence their lives. This is why the world may appear to be so out of balance. People believe it is easier to move through the world with mechanical predictability, relying heavily on rules, norms and traditions for governance, instead of creativity and spiritual truths. As a result, when observed closely, the world seems to be shifted toward the "knowing" part of you, or to the proverbial left.

I believe it's time for a paradigm shift, a shift toward the creative, toward the spirit. In keeping with that, I chose to print this book with both a literal and metaphorical "right alignment." Initially, it will seem awkward, but change/growth is always uncomfortable at first. In time, your mind and eyes will adjust.

Part 1:

crisis of thought—attachment and judgment

Human beings are perpetually insecure—constantly seeking
to be completed and validated by countless externalities.
Those externalities can be anything, from other people to
ideas. It doesn't really matter what the externalities are, our
attachment and subsequent judgment will be the same.
Therefore, the relationship between attachment and
judgment is an important one to observe, as the two are
wholly and inextricably dependent upon each other.

Chapter 1

S P A C E from Attachment:
S P A C E in Appreciation

During the quarterlife, many of us are under constant pressure to find ourselves. Finding ourselves is presented as the magic key needed to obtain all that we want and need out of life. If we want love, we must first find ourselves. If we want to be successful, we must first find ourselves. But to find ourselves we must know ourselves, and that requires developing an identity.

Our identity is comprised of all the ideas we hold close to ourselves and those we reject. It is how we define ourselves. Attachment is a natural by-product of identification, because as we identify, we simultaneously become dependent on our definition for stability. To be clear, however, attachment is about more than just developing an identity. Attachment is the psychological dependence on any thing, or set of things—be they physical items, accomplishments, or ideas—for validation. It is the thinking behind *if/then*. Meaning, *if* I possess a certain quality, or identify in a certain way, *then* I am worthy.

We attach to things by way of possession. We attach to people by way of relationships, and we attach to ideas by way of beliefs. For example, an attached person may say: I am valuable because I own a luxury car. I am important because I am the husband, wife, or daughter of so-and-so. I am righteous because of my religion. Each of the aforementioned statements can be perceived as an identity based on beliefs, but the attachment is found when we ponder how our identity makes us feel about ourselves and others. We are attached to how our beliefs about ourselves align us with some people and distance us from others.

Indeed, our associations could change and our attachment would remain just as strong. This week we may feel that we are a good person because we gave to charity. Next week we may feel we are a good person because we held our tongue instead of cursing someone. The attachment is not to the activity, it is to the belief behind the activity. We are attached to being a good person.

What is more, we believe that this goodness comes from the outside in—that it is a by-product of our relationship to an idea or person. As a result, any stimuli presented to us in contradiction to what we believe in general, will be seen as a personal attack.

And even though we may not see being a good person as a possession, anytime we identify and label, we are claiming affiliation with a certain thing. Inherent in that process is attachment. It is an identity, and we become more attached to 'who we are' than 'what we have.' This is why attachments to material things, like cars and clothes, are easier to sever.

Once we have decided on our identity, we will soon become very attached to it. Some may say, what's the big deal? Who doesn't want to be a good person? Of course we all want to be good people. And truly being a good person is not the issue. The issue is valuation (How does my identity make me feel about myself), judgment (How does my identity make me feel about other people) and separation (How does my identity make me different, better, or worse than other people).

There is nothing wrong with treating people with dignity and respect, or striving to be the best we can be in all that we undertake. But attachment isn't about treating people a certain way or doing our best; attachment is the flawed belief that happiness and wholeness are external.

Created in the image of the Universe,[2] we are divine creators, encompassing the entirety of its infinite wisdom and worth. Truly, there are no holes that need to be filled up by other people or items. There is no question of our goodness or badness as it relates to our higher selves. All things exist in the Universe, some we may judge as bad and others as good. Regardless of our perceptions, each piece creates the entirety of our experience.

---

[2] The words Universe, God, source energy, and higher self are used interchangeably throughout this text to refer to the universal consciousness present in all living beings.

attaching: the cycle

In the above paragraphs, we discovered that attachment is the clinging insecurity of predictable association. As we evaluate, we are longing to find value in ourselves. We are longing to extract this value from some thing or some person. We believe that in becoming attached or affiliated with a certain idea or person, we are adding to ourselves in some way.

Similar to identification, we begin to define ourselves by our relationship with this thing or that thing. In this way, our attachment is more about creating and sustaining our self-image than it is about the person or thing we seek to possess—it's substantiation. It makes us feel real and, more often than not, it makes us feel relevant.

Interestingly, our attachment fuels the same insecurity we are seeking to escape. At our core, we understand that anything capable of being possessed can also be lost. Many times, it is the fear of eminent loss that reinforces the attachment…and the cycle begins again. First with insecurity.

For example, if we have been attracted to men for our whole life and suddenly find ourselves attracted to a woman, we will no doubt experience a large degree of dissonance, anger, and confusion. We are not confused because of our attraction; we're confused because of our attachment to being heterosexual. Being attracted to a woman calls into question who we are, and that *cannot* be tolerated.

Consequently, we fear losing ourselves and therefore cling more closely to the ideas that we *want to possess.*

Can you see it now? The cycle? If not, here it is.

1. We feel insecure.
2. We cling more closely to our previously constructed identity, the one we have judged as pleasant.
3. We fear loss—more specifically, that other things or people will come along to threaten this identity.
4. We feel insecure about the possibility of loss, and the cycle begins again.

romantic attachment

Our attachment to people is usually by way of a relationship or role. I am a wife. I am a husband. I am a mother, etc. In romantic relationships, however, these roles oftentimes become exaggerated, causing powerful attachment.

The innate understanding that we cannot control the actions and emotions of other people causes deep feelings of insecurity and attachment. The fear of loss is almost crippling. We become attached, not only to the person, but to the idea of what this person represents. In time, we will realize that we are not really even in a relationship with the person so much as we are in a relationship with our ideas and thoughts about the person, and how those thoughts make us feel about ourselves.

During the quarterlife, the pressure to join our life with someone else's will be just as great as, if not greater than, the pressure to pursue a career. Still, I would venture to say that most people are not nearly as attached to their professional identity as they are to their personal one. It is much easier to observe fluidity in our career choice than it is within the confines of our intimate relationships.

For women, the image of the independent, but perpetually single, woman is presented as a stark reminder of what *could* happen if we don't pay close attention to what is *really* important in life. Sure, she may be a self-actualized, assertive woman, but she is also, dare I say it…single! And being coined single during the quarterlife is synonymous with being called a Puritan ice queen.

a psychological experience

On a deeper level, we must be aware that we are spirit beings having a psychological experience. In order for our psychological experience to make sense, there are certain systems that must be in place. When I say systems, I mean everything from physical laws, like gravity, to emotional abstractions, like religion. These systems keep order in our physical world. They help us make sense of what we see, feel, taste, and touch. If we were purely spirit beings, we would have no need for such systems because we would have no senses. Be careful though, because keeping order is not synonymous with keeping truth. Many of these systems are largely illusions having no real purpose aside from helping us to organize information. One such order keeping system is the mental schema. **Mental schemas** are mental structures used to organize and simplify our knowledge of the world around us[3].

They affect what we notice, how we interpret things, how we make decisions, and how we act. As such, they provide the psychological basis of both judgment and attachment. Schemas act like filters, accentuating and downplaying various elements. We use them to classify things. They also help us forecast, predicting what will happen next. We even remember and recall things via schemas, using them to translate memories.

Schemas often appear in the attribution of cause. For example, the **Multiple Necessary Causes Schema** is one where we require at least two causes before a 'fit' to the schema is declared; i.e., in order to be classified as a mammal, an animal has to have hair and produce milk.

Schemas are also self-sustaining, and will persist even in the face of disconfirming evidence. This is because if something does not match the schema, such as evidence against it, it is ignored. Such is the case when we perceive a male human. We classify male humans as mammals even though they do not produce milk.

---

[3] Robert Sternberg, *In Search of the Human Mind, 2nd ed.*, (San Diego: Harcourt Brace College Publishers, 1998).

A few examples of common schema are listed below:

- Social schemas are about general social knowledge.
- Person schemas are about individual people.
- Self-schemas are about oneself.
- Role schemas are about proper behaviors in given situations.[4]

Schemas are important because, from the time we are children, we are given the recipe for what life is supposed to look like. We form schemas from these images, and then work our whole lives trying to attain the ingredients necessary to have this life and reality.

Let's examine our schema about love. From our parents, media, and society, we learn that love is exclusive. We learn that the more we "love" someone the stricter the boundaries of our relationship should be. Schemas about marriage tell us that, in order to enjoy the benefit of this pinnacle of intimacy, we must be contractually bound to our partners. We must love them until we die and forsake all others for them. (Forsake means "to renounce or turn away from.")

When you take a moment to really look at the promise you are making, it's easy to see how much insecurity and attachment is present here. If I pledged to "turn away" from everyone else but my spouse until I died, the prospect of my

---

[4] Changing Minds. "Schema." Accessed on January 3, 2013.
http://changingminds.org/explanations/theories/schema.htm.

spouse leaving me would, understandably, be unbearable. I would want to control them, because I would want to protect myself. Wouldn't you? In our effort to control and possess, it is perfectly acceptable and realistic for us manipulate the people we love with sex, emotions, anger, money, and so on.

As the time and commitment increase, entanglement also increases and we began to feel more and more indebted to each other. We stay together out of duty and responsibility, and out of fear of letting ourselves down. Of course, we are most attached to our romantic interests because they provide us with supreme validation.

As a result, when they disappoint us or do something we do not approve of, we take it very personally. Remember our cycle of attachment? Their deviation from 'the plan' creates insecurity, so we clutch closer. In this space, there is no real love. Here, we are obsessed—we want to possess them. They are perceived as an extension of us. An appendage at best, property at worst. A healthier way to experience our partner is as a human mirror, reflecting back to us all that we are and all that we want to be. Marvel at your reflection. Love it freely, grip it softly, hold it gently, and experience it wholly.

*****

appreciation

In this text, attachment is characterized as the primary Tool of the Ego. I have characterized it this way because, in my experience, attachment provides the basis for all of the other

Tools of the Ego. It, like identification, is an anchoring characteristic of the ego. Lucky for us, the spirit also has tools—the most prominent of which is gratitude. The feeling and expression of gratitude acts as a powerful magnet, working to attract more of what we want to us. This is important because part of wanting something is first noticing that it is not *currently* there. So when we notice our energy shifting toward the negative, expressing gratitude is one of the fastest ways to regain alignment with the Universe.

Appreciation takes the act of expressing gratitude further, because, in its purest form, all gratitude requires is observation. Most humans express gratitude as a result of something either being done or being given to them. We are grateful for our jobs, our health, and our strength, as well as the people, things, and circumstances that serve us most. Appreciation, on the other hand is more subtle, more objective. Within it, there is no need to possess, to keep, or to smother. We appreciate things with a distant admiration, a detached inner bliss.

Appreciation is the slight smile that spreads across our face when we the see a field of daisies. Although we know that we will never be able to pick every daisy and take them home with us, we feel blessed just to have beheld them. In the moment, we can enjoy the experience without feeling the need to trap the feeling or find a way to duplicate it. Here there is only pleasure, only empty. S P A C E. Inside that emptiness, the rigidity of identification does not exist, only the subtle pleasure of affinity.

Affinity is defined as a natural attraction or feeling of kinship.[5] Affinity is a natural occurrence in the human experience. It's normal for us to be attracted to some things and not as attracted to others. There is no danger in having an affinity for one type of music instead of another. But the ego, in its quest to know, define, classify, and judge, takes our very natural, harmless affinity and exaggerates it, making way for attachment. Now, instead of liking rap music, we are a rap fan. Can you see the difference? Whereas one denotes an indifferent preference, the other denotes a static identity. Appreciation is the essence of that indifferent preference. Take a moment now to appreciate yourself for all that you are without any of the associations, relationships, or beliefs you have adopted.

the lesbian purist: learning to embrace my affinity

When I was nine years old I had a crush on an eighth-grade girl at my school. I begged for her to be my play-mother[6] and manufactured any excuse to be near her. She obliged, assuming I was just another one of the eager girls who admired her immense coolness. I am sure she never entertained the notion that, to me, it was more. I am also sure that she was oblivious to the fact that she was not the

---

[5] The Free Dictionary by Farlex. "Affinity." Accessed on October 11, 2011. http://www.thefreedictionary.com/affinity.
[6] At my elementary school, older girls would often take younger girls under their wing. The older girls would pretend the younger girls were their daughters. The younger girls would refer to the older girls as their, "play-mother." Having an attractive or popular play-mother was a status symbol at my elementary school.

first girl whose name I had doodled in my notebook,
adorned by rainbows and hearts.

The first girl was a girl in my summer camp. The next was
my childhood best friend. From there the list grew to include
classmates, playmates, and friends of relatives. As the years
passed, both the number of girls and the reasons I was
attracted to them increased. At seventeen, I finally allowed
my mind to explore the concept of gay-ness. And even then,
my first thought was yuck! It couldn't be that.

After all, by seventeen I had been in a three-year relationship
with a boy who I loved very much. In hindsight, I should
have become aware of the fluidity of sexuality then, but I
didn't. At seventeen there was nothing fluid about what I was
going through. All I felt was confusion and conflict. Confused
as to how I could love my boyfriend so much and still paint
the number of my favorite female basketball player and
classmate on my face. Confused at the rush I felt when she
looked at me. Confused, because my whole body seemed to
quake with anticipation and heat every time she touched me.
Conflicted, because of my commitment to my boyfriend and
to my faith. My affinity for her made it hard for me to
recognize myself. I can remember being frustrated because,
even in the midst of my uncertainty, there was no forcing in
either direction. I loved him, but I wanted her too. Bad.

By eighteen, my curiosity "grew up" to become an all out
craze. I was so distracted in class that my grades were
slipping. So, in a moment of naïve courage, I revealed my
true feelings to my secret crush. It was then that she assured

me that she "liked dick." Wow. I was heartbroken (and embarrassed), but I wasn't ready to give up.

The summer before I went off to college, behind the backs of both my parents and my boyfriend, "relief" came in the form of a scrawny White girl I met on the internet. Our affair was brief, but it was enough to move me from being curious to being bisexual.

Of course, college was another whirlwind of emotion. Being away from my boyfriend was hard, but there were plenty of other men who were interested in a girl like me. In fact, the first night I ever went to a college party, I landed one of the most sought-after guys on the scene. Still, the idea of having sex with him just wasn't appealing to me. I wasn't repulsed by it, I was just so busy being intrigued by women that I didn't have any mental space or energy left for him. I still felt comfortable dating men, entertaining them at parties and on the phone, but the sex thing—not so much. I cited my strained and tenuous relationship with my long-distance boyfriend as cause for why my sexual attraction to men didn't make the trip from high school to college. It was a lie, but it was good enough to distract me from the growing number of women I was attracted to. I was content being bisexual. Yes, happily bisexual and completely celibate.

Strangely, the idea to *become* a lesbian wasn't even mine. It was actually the idea of one of my friends (whom I also had a secret crush on). Slumped over in my bean bag chair, she shot a question at me that shattered the myth of my bisexuality.

15

"Kenya, how can you be bisexual if you never have sex with any men?" she spouted off like she was commenting on my new hairdo or the weather.

Clever as I was, I'm sure I answered her in what probably seemed like a well thought out answer. But the question gnawed at me until it, and my need to be done with the whole uncertainty of it all convinced me that I wasn't bisexual, I was gay. Wasn't it time that I picked a side anyway? Could I go through life and ride the fence like this? Yes, she was right, I was gay. That settled it. I resolved to live my life as a lesbian. I broke up with my boyfriend and went about the task of telling my friends and immediate family. I told myself that I was relieved because I was closer to knowing who I was, and that was what college, and ultimately life, was all about, right? Finding myself? I dutifully tacked *lesbian* onto the end of my list of things I knew about myself: African-American, orphaned, artistic, Aquarian…lesbian. It sounded good.

Over time, I learned that *becoming* a lesbian would be about more than just being attracted to women. I would need to choose what kind of lesbian I was. Was I a feminine lesbian, or a "femme," encompassing all the traditional roles and responsibilities of the heterosexual woman? Was I an aggressive, masculine lesbian, or a "stud," synonymous with a heterosexual man? Or maybe, I was a "stemme," the perfect mix between both. By now, I understood how this worked. I picked one, tacked it onto my list, and kept living life.

By the time I was in my mid twenties, my list included college-educated, Buddhist, writer, sorority sister, and so on. The cool thing about finding myself was that it didn't really require me to evolve at all. All I needed to do was pick up traits that fell in line with my core identity, "Black.female.lesbian." As long as there was no conflict with those three, I was good. Happy rummaging through the bag of life, picking out what I wanted and leaving behind what I didn't. But, in the quiets of my mind, there was one thing that I was having a hard time reconciling.

On the surface, I pretended that my choice to identify as a Black.female.lesbian had rid me of personal conflict. The truth was, however, this choice, along with all the other static identities I had adopted, was only intensifying the internal turmoil.

The first issue that arose centered around how being a lesbian would impact my unborn children. For years, I had known that I wanted my potential children to have a father. But deep down, I didn't think it was appropriate for me to love women and still value the energy of a man. Plus, there was a part of me that couldn't live with the fact that my children would not have a father because of a choice that I had made without their consent. Yet, this wasn't my largest concern. My largest concern was rejection from the community of lesbians that I was now a part of. I had already lost so many friends and family members as a result of my new "lifestyle" choice, and I didn't like the idea that this desire would cut me off from another group of people.

Having lost my mother at the age of twelve, I had been raised by my aunt and cousin, two women. My cousin had boyfriends, but she didn't get married until I was an adult, and my aunt had gotten divorced before I was born. Truly, there hadn't ever been any men in my life and I was, by my own estimation, successful and well balanced. Or was I? Did I feel like I wasn't balanced because I was gay? This sucked. My mind was all over the place. I needed to sort this out. I needed to be clear about what I wanted, how I was going to get it, and so on. I started writing this book before a concrete answer came to me. But, while writing the chapter about fear, I arrived at a major catharsis.

The reason why I had been unable to synthesize my thoughts about children was because, yet again, the identities I had chosen for myself were in conflict with each other. This was about me. Me and my identities. Me and my ideas. Not my children. Not my partner. My schema about children conflicted with my schema about being a lesbian. I had been taught to believe that kids should have a mother and a father, and in the back of my mind I felt limited because my father hadn't been in my life. On the other hand, my schema about being a lesbian made me feel that desiring to have a male figure in my life in any way was…I don't know, anti-lesbian.

Here I was once more, having a crisis of identity at the hands of attachment. I wondered how a self proclaimed lesbian could want to have children with a man. Being a lesbian meant loving and embracing women as well as turning away from men, completely. The other lesbian couples that I knew had children with minimal involvement from men. In extreme cases, they had forced the fathers to sign away their parental rights. They wanted no part of him and for him to have no part of the baby. If I was a good lesbian, I would adopt some semblance of this practice too. It was then that I realized how attached I was to the idea of being a lesbian.

My attachment left no room for anything other than questioning and chaos.

balance

An array of faith traditions agree, human beings were created in the image and likeness of God. God being the natural order of all things or perfect harmony. God's love is the embodiment of true love—the ultimate appreciation. It follows then, that balance is divine, with the consummate God figure encompassing both the masculine and the feminine. Since I was created in the image of this natural order, I too must possess the knowledge and potential for perfect balance. Masculinity and femininity were no exception. I was free to love whomever I wanted.

My attraction to men was simply my femininity seeking the union and balance of masculinity. But because I had chosen to turn away from all that I deemed masculine years before, my mind was unable to wrap itself around the concept. It was perfectly acceptable for me to appreciate men and masculine energy and still have an affinity for women. There was no conflict to be observed. What I wanted was balance.

Of course I loved women, what is more, I loved the woman I was with. We had a great relationship, but my love for her didn't mean I couldn't value a man. Remember the see-saw? Life is energy, and energy is balance. The perfect balance of what is perceived as good and evil, masculine and feminine and so on. The masculine energy did not have to come from a man, but if it did there was no fault to be found. Love for one does not negate appreciation of the other.

In the end, it was great to come to a place of peace on this issue, but even this was not enough for me to relegate my attachment to identifying as a lesbian. It was not until August 1, 2012, that I got a clear picture of how who I had decided to be was impacting who I really was.

an idea, an identity, an outcome

On August 1, 2012, Chick-fil-A, an Atlanta based fast-food restaurant, hosted a customer appreciation day that yielded record attendance. The customer appreciation day was initiated after Chick-fil-A president, Dan Cathy, went on record saying that he and his company supported a traditional, biblical definition of marriage. (One that included one God-fearing man and one fried-chicken-eating woman, I guess).

In any event, the result was a financial and media windfall for Chick-fil-A. Aside from all the money that was spent, there was not a lot of progress made clarifying why this traditional definition of marriage only included certain people, with certain beliefs, and certain body parts. I am still just as confused on that point as I was the day before the proverbial chicken exodus. What I am sure of, however, is that there will always be conflict when trying to make the distinction between which types of humans deserve which types of human rights.

For that reason, I didn't want to get involved in the conversation at all. But since most of the dialogue took place on social media networks—between the countless pictures, endless news coverage, and a legion of "likes" for all of the above—I almost didn't have a choice.

Everyone seemed to be in an uproar about the issue, and people were divided on everything from religion to first amendment rights.

Same-sex marriage advocates saw anyone who supported Chick-fil-A as an arch enemy, not only to same-sex marriage, but love in general. "Traditional marriage" supporters let their dollars do the talking by buying more chicken than ever before.

To counter the perceived attack of traditional marriage supporters, same-sex marriage advocates pledged to boycott the restaurant. Then they sought to shove their gay love down the throats of their opponents by hosting a national kiss day. The idea was to go to the nearest Chick-fil-A and kiss in front of their sign.

In my opinion, the whole thing was ridiculous. After a week of arguing and personal attacks, nothing good had come from any of it. All the gays had proved was that they could kiss, and all the straights had proved was that they could spend money and eat chicken.

Unfortunately, what had also been proven was how deeply rooted and profoundly powerful attachment is. This argument was not about chicken, or first amendment rights, or gay love, or a heterosexual Jesus. It was about attachment. Attachment and the division that results when people see themselves and their ideas as separate from everything and everyone else.

Plus, arguments like these only end in literal and figurative bloodshed, anyway. It usually goes a little something like the situation above. One side launches a series of personal attacks based on assumptions, attachments, and judgment, and the people on the other side of the argument do the same. A winner is determined by who can quote the most Bible verses, humiliate their opponent the most, or throw enough money at the cause for disagreement. In the end, nothing is ever done to remedy the cancer of attachment that has caused the whole misunderstanding in the first place.

I chose to title this section, "An Idea, an Identity, and an Outcome" because these three things are, on a very simple level, the root causes of every disagreement or divisive experience any of us will have. Once we have determined who we are and what we believe, we will then have to decide what that means. Eventually, what it means to be "me" will come into conflict with what it means to be "you." When this happens, a disagreement will ensue.

In addition, choosing to adopt an idea and an identity always leads to the expectation of certain outcomes in certain situations.

So with Chick-fil-A, because Dan Cathy identified with a particular religion, he felt compelled to defend his religion's definition of marriage. In addition, his identity as a member of said religion made him feel separate, not only from people who did not share his religion, but also from people who commit acts that are not acceptable within it.

His gay and lesbian opponents had a similar attachment to their sexuality. Their identity as same-sex loving people (or same-sex supporters) made them feel separate from people who do not support same-sex marriage.

So, blinded by their beliefs and identities, both sides demonstrated the cycle of attachment with textbook precision. Let's examine the cycle from the vantage point of the opponents of same-sex marriage.

1. *They felt insecure*—On some level, opponents of same-sex marriage felt personally diminished by the idea of same-sex marriage. Perhaps they felt that allowing same-sex couples to marry would threaten the definition and sanctity of their own traditional marriages. These thoughts caused deep feelings of insecurity.[7]

---

[7] It's important to note that feelings of insecurity can oftentimes mask themselves as anger.

2. *They clung more closely to their previously constructed identity*—In response, they felt the need to become more open and verbal about their beliefs. They also felt the need to convince others of their piety by presenting evidence (only from sources that were in alignment with their beliefs) to prove that they were right, and that same-sex marriage supporters were wrong. These thoughts caused them to make dangerous value judgments about people who did not share their beliefs.

3. *They feared loss*—So threatened by the idea of what same-sex marriage would mean to them, opponents lobbied to make constitutional amendments aimed at making same-sex marriage illegal. They mistakenly believed that this would rid them of their insecurity.

4. *They felt insecure about the possibility of loss, and the cycle begins again*—Understanding that making same-sex marriage illegal would not eliminate same-sex relationships or same-sex loving people, some opponents began to shift their focus from laws to religious conversions and programs aimed at disgracing and dehumanizing gays.

Steeped in anger and self-righteousness, neither group was able to see that there was no real separation between supporters of Chick-fil-A and same-sex marriage advocates.

The only real separation was the one they had constructed from their ideas and subsequent identity.

Furthermore, there was no conversation about how both religious affiliations and sexual orientations are mental constructs of a physical reality. Neither have relevance in the realm of spirit, where our true identity is found.

I am sure that both groups would agree that given the choice between love and hate, love would prevail. If more love is always good, how can either side support policies or beliefs that stifle the expression of love? When put plainly, it doesn't make much sense at all.

As I look back on this situation and the issue I discussed earlier in this chapter, I am able to see how my attachment to my race, my gender, and to my sexuality has caused a great deal of trouble in my life. It was because of these things that I had been unable to synthesize my feelings about having children and the reason I felt personally attacked by Chick-fil-A.

Deep down, I had always hated the idea that my identity as a Black.female.lesbian. reduced me to the color of my skin, what was between my legs, and who I slept with. I hated it because, although this was how I appeared and, subsequently, how I had chosen to identify, I knew myself to be so much more.

The truth is we are all so much more. So much bigger and so much more diverse than the tiny boxes we choose to squeeze ourselves into.

With this in mind, I wondered what would happen if everyone released their attachment to their ideas about what was good, bad, and righteous, and just saw people as people. I wondered if they would realize that one person's way of life does not have the power to threaten anyone else's. What is more, one person's beliefs do not have the power to change the way someone else chooses to live their life. So there is no need to feel personally attacked when someone does not agree with you. Your person is not threatened by other people's beliefs.

Legalizing gay marriage would not make me any more or less in love with my partner. It would not make me any more or any less committed to her. On the other hand, if same-sex marriage became emphatically illegal, it would not make the opponents of same-sex marriage more married, or more Christian. Changing the law would do nothing to change minds. Changing minds is something that has to happen internally. As such, it's easy to see how our attachments are not only arbitrary but irrelevant. Moreover, it's ridiculous to force your beliefs on other people simply for the purpose of keeping them from having something that you currently enjoy. Everyone deserves to be happy, and excluding one group of people from any human right is immoral in almost every faith tradition.

We live in a world where, due to the advances of modern technology and science, we can change even the most intrinsic things about ourselves. Everything from gender to skin tone can be physically altered. Men who want to be women can have a sex change. Blacks who want to be lighter can bleach their skin, and Whites can tan. Gays can marry women. Lesbians can have sex with men. Christians can convert. Married people can get divorced, and so on. How then are we so attached to how we appear physically and how we identify figuratively? It makes much more sense to change our minds about how we view, judge, and categorize other people than it does to try to fight against all that we personally disagree with.

The words *gay* and *lesbian* are simply words that denote a relationship—nothing more and nothing less. It's not who I am, it's what I prefer. It's what I have an affinity for in the same way that a religion or a political stance is. They are all choices—only as meaningful as we make them.

We are spirit beings sent to this earth to experience life in the body and the time and space continuum we occupy. We are not the collection of the ideas, opinions, accolades, preferences, and names we have accumulated. So, love who makes you happy, believe what makes you better, and do what makes a difference. It's time for us to release ourselves from the prison of our identities and make room to appreciate the whole of ourselves, both individually and as a human race.

Note to self
(and everybody else):
On Attachment

My parasitic and symbiotic attachment to my ideas and identity causes chaos and insecurity. Today, I move closer to realizing perfect balance, embracing the diversity of my affinities with sensitive awareness.

I am the transformational S P A C E of Appreciation.

Chapter 2

S P A C E from Judgment:
S P A C E in Compassion

In one of his most famous talks, the Buddha said that all
suffering is generated by the idea that we as human beings
are separate from one another. It is this flawed belief of
exclusivity and individuality that leads us to experience life
as happening to us instead of within us.

To our credit, however, it's not our fault that we experience
the world this way. From the moment we opened our eyes,
we have been taught "who we are" and "who's we are,"
(and I don't mean that spiritually). Think about it like this:
we are born to our mother and father, and because they are
the people who supply our most basic needs, namely food
and attention, we learn that we belong to them. As such, any
deviation from the ideas and values that they give to us is
seen not only as disrespectful but ungrateful. As time goes
on, we find that our parents are not the only people we
belong to. We also belong to a race, a gender, a social class,
a religion, and a sexual orientation.

In the beginning, our parents, schools, and social
organizations provide our foundation by way of control. Our
parents control our social life by exposing us to a set of adults
and children that encompass the values they want to see

develop in us. The relationships that we forge with both the ideas and people present in these circumstances, will then provide the foundation of what it means to be "who we are."

Once we have learned what it means to be "me," it will be unnecessary in later years for anyone else to make choices for us regarding how we develop or who we become. With the groundwork already laid, we will subconsciously (via our super-ego) make choices in alignment with earlier choices, without having to be told or led. Our whole life will unfold this way, and our identity will surface as the culmination of earlier choices and experiences.

What is interesting about each of the relationships listed above is that none of them arose out of a desire to separate ourselves from anyone else, but instead out of a more basic desire to get our needs for love and attention met.

So, the conversation about judgment begins here—with how our need for love and attention, and subsequent relationships to other people, places, and things cause us to identify.

who am I? the origin of identification

Identification is the tendency to internalize things and ideas about the self, thereby creating a self-image, or identity.[8]

---

[8] Eckhart Tolle, *The Power of Now: A Guide to Spiritual Enlightenment*, (Novato, Calif.: New World Library & Namaste Publishing, 2004).

Our identity is the summation of all the things we see, think, believe, have been told, or accept about ourselves. We can visualize our self-image as duffle bags full of the unique traits that we believe characterize us. Starting off, we may put our name, gender, and occupation in the bag. Digging deeper we may place our political affiliation, religion, and personal philosophy in the bag. Notice that each of the things we place in the bag denotes a relationship between "we" and "it." To illustrate this point, try pulling out a few attributes from your bag and making an "I" statement. For example, if I reach into my bag, my statement may sound like this: My name is Kenya and I am a thirty-year-old African-American woman. This statement is a snapshot of how I view myself, it's my identity.

As we examine the contents of our bag, we will begin to notice that deep within what we *are* is what we *are not*. In stating, believing, and observing what "I am," I am also observing what "I am not." And because the *self* is the frame of reference for most people, every relationship, conversation, or interaction that we have will now be filtered through the lens of our identity.

Now observe how your identity makes you feel. Does your identity make you feel good? For most people it does, and that's understandable. Indeed, our relationships to things and people create a sense of belonging, and we all want to belong. In an ironic cosmic twist, many people work just as hard trying to establish an idiosyncratic identity as they do to find a place to express this identity with others who identify similarly. Meaning, we all want to be different—just like everyone else!

It follows that the people, places, and things that bear the closest resemblance to "me" will be seen as pleasant or familiar, whereas the people who do not identify as I do will be seen as foreign, different, and possibly a threat. They are not like "me." They do not understand "me." They are different and therefore undesirable. Our desire to cling to what is pleasant and to separate ourselves from what we consider unpleasant will permeate every decision that we make. Witness the birth of judgment.

We judge because the integrity of our *idea* of self is rooted in identification with ideas, concepts, roles, or material things. We judge because inherent in our puffed up or deflated view of ourselves is a predisposition to place things in order of value using our image of self as the rubric. We want to be superior, right, righteous, nice, good, or any other attribute that we view as pleasant. We will therefore place mental and physical distance between ourselves and anything and anyone who does not meet our idiosyncratic criterion for worthiness.

Although people can be intensely connected to their material objects, I would argue that our connection and identification with those non-material aspects of ourselves, such as ideas and opinions, are even more deeply ingrained in our identity. As a result, it is easy to become defensive when our precious ideas and concepts are challenged. As we perceive another person's approval as validation, their disapproval, even if unspoken, is intolerable. So when disagreements arise, we feel attacked as if we need to defend our point, our idea, ourselves. It can seem as if the mere fact that we exist is in question. Our relationships can then become combative or competitive. Differences among people can become a breeding ground for the most dangerous type of judgment—prejudice.

equality and sameness

Now that we have established that identity and separation are the two main ingredients in judgment, let's take a moment to examine what happens when we allow these two phenomena to progress unchecked.

After our initial observation that other people and their ideas are separate from us, the ranking and ordering begins. So not only is the other person and their stuff different or separate from me, but they are also better or worse than me and my stuff.

This thought process has created the idea that equality equals sameness. Meaning that, in order to be given equal rights or consideration, one person has to prove that they are the same as the other.

It is easy to observe this happening time after time throughout history as groups have fought for equality. One need only study the events of the Civil Rights Movement, the Women's Suffrage Movement, and the more recent

Human Rights Campaign to see how Blacks, women, and homosexuals have worked to prove their equality by denying any trace of dissent from the majority. Unfortunately, in the midst of the fight to gain equality (which is really a fight for validation from the majority group); the need to assimilate commonly arises.

For instance, after being forced to abandon their language, religion, and traditions, African-Americans began going to great lengths to speak, appear, and behave like their captors. They developed a strong sense of assimilation, and now, although the pressure to assimilate has greatly decreased, the desire is still strong among some.

Homosexuals are currently in the midst of a similar fight as they struggle for the right to marry. One need only glance at the homosexual community to see how hard many of its members work to mimic the heterosexual world.

Gays and lesbians commonly use words and adopt practices that purposefully mirror heterosexual relationships. Words like *top* and *bottom* for men or *femme* and *stud* for women are used to distinguish who is the girl or boy in the relationship. Domestic responsibilities are often also divided in ways that are traditionally masculine and feminine.

I guess the supposition is that once the straight world sees gays as the same, they will feel enough pity to grant them the right to marry. But beneath the fight to marry, there is a more human desire to be accepted.

34

Gays, like Blacks, like women, were and are merely searching for a connection, a sense of belonging. They mistakenly feel that once the majority group grants this approval by way of rights or a "pat on the back," they will feel full and whole. This is yet another trick of the ego, because the desire to belong and affiliate is not unique to minority groups.

All of us can remember what it felt like when we got our first rejection letter from the company we always wanted to work for, or how we felt when the sorority we rushed did not call us back for an interview. Now try to imagine what it would feel like if that sorority were the world or a sector of society as a whole. How alienated do you feel now? Can you imagine blaming yourself, trying to figure out what it is about you that is so undesirable? Being able to imagine this feeling is the beginning of compassion.

Wisdom teaches us that there is only one world and that our identities have more to do with perceptions than with reality. Wisdom helps us to recognize that the energy that beats our heart, beats the heart of every man, woman, child, dog, and cat, and it is the same energy that grows trees and nourishes flowers. We are alive, and we are each an extension of source energy. Therefore, any differences that we observe among us are largely aesthetic. In all the ways that matter, we are equal…even if we are not the same.

It's important to note that we can still celebrate our individuality without being judgmental. There is no need to put on a black robe and place all the qualities that make you unique under a proverbial blanket. The beauty of compassion is that it doesn't require that. Indeed, compassion can lead us to feel better about ourselves than ever before, because in it we grow to realize that our beauty is not compromised by the beauty of another—it's enhanced.

*****

Compassion

God, the universal consciousness, has the power to know not only the truth of who we are but also the way in which we process information. Our higher self understands that although we are one of many manifestations of source energy, we frequently forget this fact. It also knows that our primary means to synthesize information is through the singular lens of self. Me. It follows that in order for true empathy to evolve, one must see other people through that same lens. From this idea the golden rule was born.

"Do unto others as you would have them do unto you" is the essence of compassion.

Yet, true compassion goes beyond a cliché and a worn out Bible verse. It compels us to truly identify with other people, dispelling the myth of separation that taints our perception.

My idea of me is the standard by which others are measured. The danger here is that most of us have no clue who we are, because we are defining ourselves with things and ideas that do not capture our fundamental nature. They are more like possessions than attributes. If we knew our true nature, we would find no value in arbitrarily separating ourselves from other people. In reality, we are all the infinite, timeless, endless, immortal empty. S P A C E. Any other identity only limits and alienates. Compassion arises when we see that physical, aesthetic, and perceptual separation doesn't denote spiritual separation.

We are all the products of source energy. Therefore, any human suffering should be seen as personal suffering. We do not need to compare and argue. Truly, all interaction is, or should be an exchange of energy. Our parasitic attachment to our opinions and ideas is simply the product of our flawed and limited view of ourselves. Our judgment is a symptom that the parasite is winning.

I see you shining!

For the majority of my life, I was raised by my aunt and cousin, both devout Christian women. I can remember them telling me to *be* a blessing to other people. They would tell me to be the person who holds the door open for the next person to enter, to leave an extra quarter in the meter when I drove away, to smile at strangers, and to speak up when someone is being verbally assaulted. What could it hurt? From them I learned how important it is to be mindful of my influence on others. Then, I didn't recognize that they were teaching me compassion, but now I understand.

Nature is always inclusive and objective, and therefore creates the best illustration of the overall folly of judgment. Let's consider the sun. The sun, even though its position is physically fixed, has the capacity to touch an infinite number of people, places, and things. It has the power to warm bodies, tan skin, grow plants, and so on. Why? Because of its rays. The sun's rays are what we feel.

Human beings can be likened to the sun's rays. We are the *way* in which the world experiences God. We are the *how* of the *what*. God moves through us as individuals and as a whole. Similar to the sun's rays, some of us will choose to direct our shine in different places. Think about it like this: although Alaskans do not get as much sun as Floridians do, residents of each place have the benefit of feeling and experiencing the sun in some capacity. Comparably, everyone whose life we touch will enjoy the benefit of knowing God in us and through us. My aunt, cousin and mother were those rays for me, even though I didn't realize it.

> Even
> After
> All this time
> The sun never says to the
> earth
> "You owe
> me"
> Look
> What happens
> With a love like that
> It lights the
> Whole
> Sky.
>
> -Hafiz

If we begin to see ourselves as extensions of God, some of us will have to take a hell of a lot more responsibility for what we say and do. For instance, remember when you were a kid and your mother would remind you each morning that you'd better be on our best behavior because you were representing her? I do, and it terrified me. I would never want to embarrass my mother, the woman who gave me life and for whom I had so much respect.

I try to apply this same principle when I think of myself now. Not only am I the only child of Gwen Jackson, but I am the human manifestation of God. Whew! Strangely, this thought isn't intimidating. The concept is exciting. I know that it was the kindness of my aunt and cousin that drove me to seek the path of spiritual enlightenment. I also know that it was my mother's intelligent wit and humor that gave me the relatability to do so. I was a seed, nurtured by the warmth of each of these women.

I am filled with gratitude for all that they have given me and want more than anything to return the favor. There are so many seeds in the world waiting to be nurtured and cultivated by your mind, love, and light. This is impossible if you are constantly picking and choosing who deserves the right to know, feel, and see you. How dare you shield another from your shine!

Finally, a lesson in exclusivity from our friend the sun. Let's get practical here. The next time you get ready to judge someone else, think of how our lives would change if we experienced nature the same way we experience our personal relationships. What if water only nourished the skinny, beautiful and educated? Sure, everyone could drink it, but it wouldn't provide the same nutrition to everyone. Doesn't that somehow seem unfair? Cruel, even? Yet, we are more than comfortable accepting that certain people deserve more money, more success, and more happiness. However, when we use an example like water, somehow it is easier to see how unfair any unequal allocation of resources really is. In complete defiance of nature, man has created a defective, egoic system of resource allocation based on a fabricated and narrow view of the self. Lucky for us, the resources that we need most, those given to us by God makes no distinction as to who to give what.

So let's be patient with ourselves and each other. We have all been taught the same flawed mindset. It has taken a lifetime for us to assimilate all the many attachments and judgments we subscribe to, it will likely take time for us to change those thoughts. In the meantime commit to working toward seeing the *GOoD* in everybody.

In a glass house (throwing stones): the process of affiliating

My struggle with judgment peaked in my early twenties. In hindsight, I think this happened because it was then that I was most sensitive about who I was. I desperately wanted to maintain the persona that I had created for myself in earlier years. After college, this was harder to do because I didn't have the predictability of school to anchor me. I wasn't the president of some club or the top student in my class. I was just another twenty-something graduate—one among hundreds of thousands.

Of course, it was really my insecurity that caused me to be so judgmental, but at the time I wasn't ready to hear that. It was better to believe that anyone who criticized me was a "hater" or jealous of me. I mean, of course they were jealous of me. I

was beautiful, educated, and full of potential. It was plain to
see how much better I was than everyone else! Right?

As I collected accolades and the subsequent compliments
that came with them, I mentally widened the distance
between me and other people. I would gossip about people,
recounting all the mistakes they had made in their lives and
convincing myself that I was way too smart to do the same.
It was safe and easy in my cocoon of judgment…that is,
until I became "one of them."

In the winter of 2007, the contract on my seasonal job ran
out and I found myself unemployed for seven months.
Simultaneously, my relationship of three years ended
abruptly. In a matter of months, I went from being in love
and gainfully employed to being nearly homeless and
completely alone. I tried a variety of different employment
paths, but nothing panned out.

In June, I got a notice from my apartment complex. I was
being evicted. I wasn't surprised. I hadn't been able to
maintain the $950-per-month rent for the past three months.
The only money that I was earning was $130 a week from
my unemployment benefits, and that was commonly eaten
up in overdraft fees.

I can remember buying a one-gallon gas can and putting it in
the trunk of my car because I ran out of gas so much. I only
needed a one-gallon can because I never had more than five
or ten dollars to put in my tank anyway. It was hard.

Desperate only half describes how I felt, because, in addition to having no money, I also had no one in my life to support me emotionally. There was no one to pat me on the back and say that things would be ok. No one to hold me and make me feel whole, human.

My mind constantly swirled in circles, and insomnia held hostage any remnant of peace I may have had. Looking back, I am surprised I didn't check my pillow for brain matter, because I was certain that I was losing my mind with each passing day.

Before this time, I had never considered myself a materialistic person. Probably because, for the most part, all of my friends were poor during college and graduate school. It was acceptable for me to eat Ramen noodles and play "eenie-meenie-minie-moe" with my bills because I was in school and I had potential. I was still a member of the educated elite for a while. After school, things changed. My friends got jobs and they had money. I, on the other hand, would spend hours clutching my cell phone, silently chanting, begging for it to ring with a job opportunity on the other end. Nothing happened. Nothing except depression. I watched myself move from "most likely to succeed" to "an utter disappointment," in a matter of months.

Then I met a girl at a local night club.

She was pretty. We started to talk and almost immediately began to bond. She shared with me that she was in transition too, having just moved to Atlanta from Colorado. We spent our days recounting past times of happiness with distant nostalgia. It wasn't long before she got a job bartending at an adult entertainment nightclub. As the bartender, she could see how much the cocktail waitresses were making, and she encouraged me on a daily basis to apply. I was intrigued, but nervous. A strip club! A strip club in Atlanta? Not to mention this was and still is one of the most popular strip clubs in Atlanta. So, in truth, it was not *a* strip club in Atlanta, it was *the* strip club in Atlanta (which made me even more nervous).

The manager looked me up and down before telling me that I could start the next Thursday. What unfolded in front of me was almost surreal. My life became a sordid mix of a reality television show and a gangster rap video—replete with the money, the women, the sex, the drugs, and the violence.

The money came easy, $300 to $400 dollars on a normal night and up to $1,000 when there was a special event in town. Within a month, I could see a light at the end of my tunnel.

I became obsessed with the money. So obsessed, that I pushed my feelings of shame about working at a strip club deep down. If I were honest with myself, I was completely horrified that I worked in a strip club. All I could do to secure myself was to notice all the things about my co-workers that separated me from them, and to constantly remind myself of all the many ways that I was different and, most importantly, better than them.

I started with my education. I had a Master's degree. I was just doing this in the meantime. This was not going to be my career.

After the judgment, came the pity. I felt so bad for them, for having to do what they were doing. Never once did I entertain the notion that I was just as much a part of the industry as they were. Sure I wasn't giving ten-dollar table dances or pasting plastic eyelashes to my face, but this was my life too.

I ignored the fact that I found myself wearing far more make-up than usual, cutting slits down the front of my shirt and wearing footless tights more suitable for underwear than pants.

Without a doubt, I worked very hard not to see myself as part of their world, but, after a while, I just couldn't deny it anymore. I had become addicted to the money and the lifestyle. I craved it. Even on my days off, I was in the club. I even became a regular at other strip clubs in the city. I lost my sensitivity to the disrespectful, sexually charged music. My own sexual appetite increased as I started to see myself exhibiting the same characteristics of the ladies I had once felt so separate from.

I spoke about women with distance and objectivity. I picked up girls with the sole intention of using them for sex or status or both. I paraded them, one by one, in the club and shot playful winks to my co-workers, broadcasting my intentions with clarity.

Beyond that, every man I saw was a customer. I leveraged my affiliation with the club to gain free entry and VIP treatment at other night clubs. I even bragged to my friends about the celebrities and drug dealers that I had the pleasure of knowing.

I didn't tell them how degrading it was to go to work with my breast pushed up and my face painted, and to smile at the faces of men who thought that a stack of one dollar bills made them invincible. Truthfully, to them I was just as expendable as the women on stage. It didn't take long before the men began to proposition me. They would ask me for my phone number, try to take me out on dates, and offer me money for my time and company. I never obliged them, but I definitely considered it on many occasions.

As I started to identify more and more with my evening surroundings, the distance between me and the "real" job, I had acquired two weeks after starting at the club grew. Once the sole subject of my prayers, my day job became an unwanted chore that I resented. I hated the stuffy predictability of it. I hated the complacent drones posing as humans that worked alongside me. Them, with all their religious and social conformity, and me, with all my youth and unbridled freedom. I decided that I was different and better than them too.

The lure of the club was real, and the line that I had drawn between me and the girls thinned. How different was I, really? I too counted dirty money on the floor of my apartment. I too endured the shame of taking handfuls of dollar bills to the bank, where the teller looked at me with jealously and the exact same judgment that I did the girls I worked with. The women were selling themselves, and so was I.

sold

There is one incident in particular that stands out in my mind as a pivotal moment in my experience with judgment and compassion. It happened almost four years ago, when my roommate invited me to attend an exclusive party with her and a friend. The party was for a popular basketball player and promised to bring out all of the "ballers," big spenders, and bottle poppers. At the time, this was my type of party.

My excitement was tempered with fear however, because despite earning over $1,000 a week, I still struggled with my appearance. In my head, I thought I was sure to be the darkest, ugliest thing in the building that night.

My roommate and her friend, both models, looked beautiful and were soon invited to go into the ultra super-secret VIP lounge located in the basement of the club. In the super-secret lounge, the players and their wives were all lined up in their respective sections, drinking and partying. The women looked liked they had stepped off the cover of some men's magazine, each with perfect hair, a perfect body, and perfect clothes. You can imagine that being in this environment made me feel beyond self-conscious. I felt like I was going to suffocate. I had to get out of there—to do something to make myself feel better.

In that moment, I cut my eyes across the floor and saw one of my most loyal customers from the strip club. He recognized me and I sauntered right over. Even though I was only interested in escaping from what felt like the glaring scrutiny of the women in the super secret VIP sections, he was much more interested in my outfit for the evening. He didn't waste any time commenting on my formfitting sweater dress. I can remember him remarking that he'd had no clue what I looked like in regular clothes. He even alerted the other members of his party to the reality of my physique. In fact, he was so impressed with my body that he asked me if I would get his drinks for the remainder of the night. *Ummm...ok*, I thought. (Here, I pause to remind you that we were in the super secret VIP area, where each section had its own waitress).

This fact seemed to escape him. He said he wanted to watch me get the drinks, (another compliment to my body, I guess). Feeling increasingly self-conscious I agreed. He gave me a $100 bill and ordered one drink. When I returned with his change he took it, only to slide it into my cleavage and wink.

Three years later, it's hard to tell this story because I can see how cheap and degrading it was. But in the moment, I needed it. I was happy to report to my roommate that drinks were on me for the rest of the night. Not that she needed any more. By the time I got back to her, she was already refusing drinks from the army of admirers that were sending them to her. Unwilling to acknowledge how I really felt, I was comfortable with my body getting me what her beauty had gotten her. I even smacked my teeth at the jealous waitress, who saw the whole situation. I can remember being so excited about the exchange that I didn't hesitate to tell the girl I was dating as soon as I got in the car. Her response was sobering.

She asked me if having that guy and his friends stare at me all night was worth the $88 I was left with. She asked how I felt to take money out of the other waitress's pocket. She wondered how I would feel if someone did that to me. It was then that I allowed myself to acknowledge the depth of my addiction to a life that I had once so vehemently sought distance from. Her comments stung me, and planted the seed that would ultimately grow into compassion.

On a deeper level, I realized that placing distance between myself and the girls at the club had done nothing for my own self-esteem. I was still just as vulnerable to the pretty girls physically, as I had once been to my friends financially. What I wanted was to feel whole, and there was no amount of money that was going to give me that feeling. It didn't matter what type of affiliations I claimed, there would always be those places that I wouldn't feel a part of, even when I was physically allowed to enter them. I had judged a group of women, and now being a part of that very group was the only thing that mattered to me. It became the validation that I needed. It had become my new identity.

The truth was, I was a glorified admin at my day job with far more responsibility than I had authority, and in the evening I

was a waitress. *That* was the truth. I had created this façade
as a coping mechanism to secure myself.

My whole life, I had been led to believe that my value rested
in who I was and what I did. When what I did didn't fit the
image of who I wanted to be, first I judged, then I changed
my image to accommodate my new circumstance.

It was a low point for me, but from it came some of my
most valuable lessons. The first lesson was that the moment
we judge someone else, we are simultaneously judging
ourselves. It wasn't the girls at the club who made me feel
bad about working there. It wasn't my friends or family who
felt like I was failing because I had lost my job. It was me. I
judged myself, and in doing so I created my own personal
mental hell.

The second lesson was that identity is fluid. And if identity
was as fluid (as I now knew it to be), I had the psychological
capability to see myself as anyone. There was something in
me that resonated with everyone I came in contact with. I
also learned that personal affiliations have as much to do
with proximity and circumstance as they have to do with
choice. Circumstance had placed me in close proximity with
a world I didn't even know existed. Over time, it had
become so close to me that I absorbed it into my self-image,
and therefore chose to judge it less harshly.

I began to see myself in the faces of those women, and
compassion emerged. I empathized with the women, instead
of feeling the cold indifference of sympathy. I understood,

because it was me. I knew how cheap it felt to be desired only for my body, and I also knew that sometimes negative attention can feel better than no attention at all. Who was I to judge them? I didn't want people to look down on me because I worked in a strip club. I wasn't a bad person. I wasn't a slut, and neither were the women I worked with. A lot of the girls had children or family members to support. And even if they didn't, couldn't I understand what it felt like to believe I had nothing more to offer the world than my body?

We all find ways to evaluate ourselves, be it with our appearance or with our accolades and degrees. We look for ways to quantify our worth and then go out into the world with it strapped to our forehead as an identity. In essence, we are saying, "I am worthy because…." But in truth, we are simply searching. Searching for our place in the world, using whatever asset we deem to be most appropriate for our current place and situation.

During the quarter-life, we will be asked tough questions. Questions of value and identity. If we are not careful, we will allow society to answer for us, and we will judge.

Of course, there are certain occupations and affiliations that are a better fit for some people. But, having had years of experience in corporate America, I can testify that you don't need to swing on a pole to feel cheap. Furthermore, the moment we feel that we have the right to judge another person's path, the Universe will get to work showing us just how easy it is to fall from glory.

Upon leaving my job at the strip club in the summer of 2008, I vowed to remember this fact. I kissed my friends goodbye and whispered a heartfelt thank you to the Universe for showing me that there is beauty and wisdom everywhere. I would never find my worth in the mental distance that I placed between me and other people, because my worth wasn't in the separation. It was in the wisdom of connectivity.

Now whenever I find myself slipping into a judgmental mind, I try to channel the energy of past spiritual leaders, the energy of Jesus, Buddha, and Mohammed. I imagine how patient and compassionate each would have had to be in order to minister to the diverse audiences they sought to teach. How important was it that they refrained from alienating their followers with judgment and an attitude of arrogant superiority. Indeed each delivered a message that assured followers that the greatness they saw in their spiritual leader resided within them as well.

I am here to remind you of the same.

Note to self
(and everybody else):
On Judgment

When I judge, I separate myself from the
power and security of source energy.
Compassion strengthens my relationship
with other spirit beings and therefore
brings me closer to the realization of
universal connectivity.

I am the unifying S P A C E of Compassion

Part 2:

crisis of action-fear and destruction

Fear is a manifestation of the accumulated attachments and judgments that we have deemed unpleasant or unwanted. It prevents us from thinking and behaving in ways that are not in alignment with previously accepted attachments and judgments. Indirectly our inability to move outside of our comfort zone causes us to become destructive. We destroy the possibility of all that we could be by clinging so closely to all that we have decided or been told to be.

Chapter 3

S P A C E from Fear:
S P A C E in Enthusiasm

This chapter has been, by far, the hardest chapter to write. It has been revised countless times and ignored far more than that. First, it was the longest, then the shortest. Eventually, it just became the dreaded chapter I had to write in order to finish the book. I have scraped it several times and have even cut pieces of it out to be placed in other chapters. Quite frankly, it has been a monster of an undertaking to be honest enough to write about fear. And not just for the obvious reasons like I am afraid to face my fears, but for less evident ones, like sometimes the fear seems so big I can't explain it.

I have experienced fear on so many levels and in so many areas of my life, that it's been hard to narrow it down into a clean-cut chapter or a story. While I am writing this, I am forcing myself to be ok with that, because a major part of my personal experience with fear surrounds acceptance and worthiness.

If I had to pin it down, I would say my deepest fear is that I am somehow unworthy of being accepted. And since my work hinges heavily on how other people feel about me, my fear of not being accepted grew into a larger fear of not being successful. I plan to go into more detail about that later, but first let's begin our conversation by talking about what fear is, what it isn't, and how it affects us.

Fear *is* a powerful motivator.

In fact, I would venture to say that fear is the most powerful motivator of them all. Meaning that the majority of the decisions we make, both those that we deem bad and those that we deem good, are rooted in fear. We have a fear of failure. We have a fear of being accepted. We have a fear of going to hell or displeasing God. We have a fear of disappointing our parents and friends. A fear of growing old alone, and so on and so on.

Fear is a big deal, and unlike the other Tools of the Ego, which are more or less negative thought patterns, fear is much more. It's a negative thought pattern that leads to a collection of negative emotions like lack, unworthiness, and immobility. These negative emotions can then take root in our lives and become our dominant life experience. Because of this, fear is one of the most dangerous Tools of the Ego, second only to destruction.

Fear is dangerous because it is the only Tool of the Ego that equally impacts both what we think and what we do. It not only affects our mind, it affects our mobility. Think about it, even when you feel deeply attached to an idea, an identity, or an outcome, you still have that ability to move forward. But a mind poisoned by fear is almost completely immobile.

When you are afraid, you procrastinate. When you are afraid, you do not participate. When you are afraid, you do not pursue. Because you are afraid, you either do nothing at all or only that which you have done in the past. Fear keeps us trapped in the predictable, completely unable to step into the paradise that we both desire and deserve.

Fear *is not* a root Tool of the Ego, like attachment or judgment.

Root Tools of the Ego are direct consequences of identification. Meaning anyone who chooses to identify in any way will experience attachment and judgment almost immediately after. Fear, on the other hand, results only after one has first attached to an idea and judged an outcome.

The question remains then, if fear is not a root Tool of the Ego and therefore not a consequence of identification, how did we become fearful in the first place? The answer is found in an unlikely place. Fear comes from the destruction of confidence.

the introduction of failure, the origin of fear

I'd like to think that self-confidence is gained by completing tasks, facing fears, and emerging unscathed. When one looks at a challenge and finds oneself able to navigate through it, one not only begins to trust one's ability more, but also to be less fearful of new challenges. When we trust ourselves, we are confident. We are enthusiastic about life and all that it offers, but when we do not trust ourselves we are fearful...of everything.

The interesting thing about trusting ourselves is that it isn't something that we must learn to do. More often than not, it is something that we unlearn over time. Think about it, as children we feared nothing. We felt perfectly safe walking off the edge of a table or putting anything in our mouth that would fit. We had no concept of danger—or mortality, for that matter. We trusted ourselves to do whatever we put our mind to. We thought we could do anything from revive dead animals to fly. We thought we were superhuman. It was only after countless times of being told "no," "stop," "don't" by the people we trusted that we learned failure was an option. And once we knew that failure was an option, we learned not to trust our own judgment. We began to entertain the notion of our own fallibility, and for many of us, a fear of failure has permeated every other life decision from that point on.

Ultimately, as we aged, fear was introduced as a necessary by-product of caution or safety. We were told what people, places, decisions, and activities were safe. Safe decisions were the ones that were sure to result in a certain outcome. Safe activities were the activities that had already been done and that did not have the capacity to hurt or disappoint us. Even if they did not make us happy, we were safe, and to a fearful mind, safety is more important than anything else.

Most of us were also taught that it was our unsafe and illogical decisions that caused negative things to happen.

Indirectly, this taught us to blame ourselves when bad things happened. Now, we think it's our fault when we don't get the right job or can't create the right relationship. We rationalize that, in order to be successful, all we need to do is make better, safer decisions.

It is the combination of these misinterpreted life experiences that erode our confidence. They keep us locked in a rote routine and cause us to be fearful of the greatness that we so desperately want. So when we say that we fear our greatness, what we are really saying is we fear what we have never seen, and what we no longer trust ourselves to achieve. Moreover, since we have not allowed ourselves to experience the greatness within us in such a long time—we begin to feel that it no longer exists.

That's why the quarterlife crisis is so riddled with fear. Because, for the first time in our lives, we start to notice how much different the agreements we have made as adults are from what we believed as children. We struggle to blend the two realities, and a crisis of identity (attachment and judgment) and ability (fear) result.

We begin to rationalize that happiness is something we have to earn or be deserving of. Then, in the struggle to prove that we *do* deserve it, fear shows up in a variety of ways.

I chose to experience my fear by way of anxiety. You know that nagging apprehension mixed with nervousness type of feeling? The fear was paralyzing at times. For years, I told myself I was afraid to fail. But honestly, the perpetual cycle of failing and starting over again had become more predictable than anything else. Plus, part of me felt like I needed to go through trials in order to be worthy of happiness. I soon learned that I was wrong. We are all worthy of happiness. We are all worthy of having everything we expect to have. But first, we must stop blaming ourselves for our failures and start taking responsibility for our success.

Now, for some, fault and responsibility may seem synonymous, but they are not. Fault is the passive assignment of negative emotions like blame and guilt. Responsibility, on the other hand, comes from a place of power and is rooted in the promise of transcendence. You are *assigned* blame, but you *take* responsibility. Taking responsibility for our success begins with taking responsibility for our thoughts, more specifically our expectations.

expect the "bads," fear the "goods."

Conventional wisdom tells us to expect the best but prepare for the worst. Well, if we are prepared for the worst, what will we do when the best happens? It's almost like disappointment is the default emotion instead of the backup plan. For example, have you ever caught yourself secretly frowning when you heard good news from a friend or loved one? Talking negatively about your friends' new relationship, listing all the reasons it won't last? Or telling people, "it's great that you bought a new car, but you know it's going to kill you in maintenance?" Sounds terrible, doesn't it? Yet, all of us can identify with one or more of these scenarios.

It's okay though, take it easy on yourself. You are not the only one who feels this way. Many of us feel a little uncomfortable when listening to good news. Especially if we don't have anything cool going on in our own lives. If we did, at least we could engage in some competitive banter with our friends to make ourselves feel superior to them. However, behind this song and dance is our real fear. Fear of what we don't know. Fear of what we can't define. It's the fear of happiness.

I'll be honest—I don't know many happy people. I can't pick up the phone and call a list of happy people and hope to hear happy stories about their happy lives. Not that all of my friends are suicidal Debbie downers. They just all live in the real world and have real-world problems. Their problems cause them to see their real-world experience as one of sacrifice and harsh realities. Sadly, the harsh reality of the real world doesn't leave much room for genuine happiness from within.

As adults, most times, even our fleeting moments of happiness are due to an external situation. So really, in those moments our happiness is more so a product of attachment and judgment, than it is true happiness. True happiness is some distant utopian ideal, like an end to world hunger. Most of us want it and even pray for it, but deep down we don't really believe it's possible, which is why we delay it.

We tell ourselves we will be happy when this or that happens, when we get this particular thing, or turn this age. We say we will definitely be happy when we get a raise at work or meet that special someone. Perhaps when we have our first child or run our first marathon? In the meantime, we become content with the dormant misery that underlies our daily lives.

We expect to hate our job, to endure fights in our relationships and disappointments from friends. We decide early on that other people aren't trustworthy and that the only person we can rely on is ourselves. That is, until we become old, cancerous, and die. It's amazing how many horrible things we accept about life on a daily basis.

With the prospect of goodness so easily dismissed, we have to ask ourselves, what are we truly afraid of? If we are willing to invite the lions, tigers, and bears of this life into our living rooms, then we are not afraid of bad things. We expect them. In the popular book and movie, *The Secret,*[9] multiple scientists stated that what we expect, we ultimately invite. So it follows, that if we are comfortable inviting bad things into our experience by virtue of our expectations, then our true fear is not bad things.....it's good things.

Human beings are products of our environments, and our environments are products of the collective consciousness. If our collective consciousness is shrouded in an expectation of negativity, our environments will reinforce what we are thinking and expecting. The only way to change our experiences is to change our minds. What our minds need is

---

[9] Byrne, Rhonda, "The Secret," DVD.

a new focus to anchor our thoughts. In the case of fear, we need only focus our minds on the opposite, enthusiasm.

fear of failure: the dark cloud beneath the silver lining

Now that we understand where fear comes from, let's get into some specifics about one of the most prevalent fears we will experience as quarterlifers: the fear of failure.

During the early twenties, most of our thoughts are centrally focused on one thing—success. More specifically, money. For many of us, money and success are like conjoined twins: merged at the hip, separate, but desperately dependent on each other for survival. As a result, money becomes the means by which we measure ourselves. It is the physical representation of our self-worth. When we have no money, we feel worthless.

After all, the whole "go to school" thing is largely attractive because we *think* that it will ultimately lead to more opportunities and more money. Unfortunately, what meets most graduates is something a bit less idealistic. In a flash, we are pretty much evicted from the comforts of our dorm room or subsidized housing and forced to find lodging in the real world. (It's expensive). Our friends move away, and our reduced-cost meal plan is revoked. (We're hungry and lonely). Sixth months later, our loan providers start calling, wanting their money back. (We don't have it).

The prognosis for those of us who graduated during the recession is even grimmer, because many of us were unable to find a job at all. And the few of us who did, did not start out earning the type of money that we anticipated. Soon, we began to notice our wealth of potential dwindling, and we started to feel eminent failure inching up and tickling our necks.

Certainly there were some people who did not have this experience. Some found jobs right out of college and will never have to worry about money again. But for many of us, money will become an issue, and when money becomes an issue a whole slew of issues follow it—issues like jealousy, depression, and apathy.

As we receive rejection letters or observe our funds decreasing, a great fear sets in our spirits. This fear separates us from the life that we want, and we forget how hard we worked in school. We forget how successful we were *supposed* to be and focus solely on what is *not* happening in the present. If a great deal of time passes, we may begin to fear that we will never get the right job or will never live up to our goals. It can become crippling.

However, behind this fear of failure, and behind all fear for that matter, is a deeper issue that was mentioned earlier. It is the fear of, "being good enough" or "deserving." My Science of Mind teacher, David Ault, calls this feeling worthiness.

Worthiness is the feelings and thoughts that make us believe we should get the things we want. They are the feelings of trust, confidence, and happiness that make us feel valuable and deserving. The problem is, since we were children we have been taught to attach our feelings of worthiness to external situations and stimuli. Things like our grades, the opinions of other people, and our ability to make safe decisions. Accordingly, many of us feel a diminished sense of self-confidence, and therefore find it difficult to face the complications of life without those things or people. In essence, we have lost faith in own abilities, developed a tarnished opinion of ourselves, and an inflated opinion of other people. As a result, we seek someone or something to make ourselves feel of strong, fortified, ready, and able.

The truth is, our worthiness is not dependent on any of these things. It is not dependent on our relationships, our jobs, or any of the other identifications we have adopted. We are worthy simply because we are. Sadly, many of us think worthiness, like happiness is something we need to work for or earn.

Consequently, as students we thought that since we were working toward something, we deserved all the good that would eventually come to us. We were even comfortable delaying our financial independence because we believed that our hard work would pay off. We worked hard and long and were expecting to receive results. For this reason and others, many of us may have never experienced extreme issues of worthiness prior to college graduation.

You see, before this time, there had always been a series of tiny victories along the way, each one reinforcing our worthiness and impending success. Imagine all the graduation ceremonies, milestone birthdays, and college acceptance letters that we received before we came to this place. Our parents were proud and so were we. We felt like we deserved it and our pride carried us through college and perhaps even graduate or trade school. That is, until our first real brush with disappointment. It was then that the uncertainty began. Suddenly, with no ceremonial recognition of worthiness to look forward to, and now without the encouragement of those small victories, we slip into a period of questioning.

This period of questioning is the crux of the quarterlife crisis, and it is the perfect incubator for fear. Abby Wilner, the author who coined the term *quarterlife crisis*, defines it as "the period of anxiety, uncertainty, and inner turmoil that often accompanies the transition to adulthood." While there have been countless books, blogs, and websites developed to dissect this subject, one key truth is missing in all of them. Fear.

In reality, the quarterlife crisis is an accumulation of fear surrounding long-standing ideas about success, relationships, and identity, and how those ideas undermine our confidence and subsequent feelings of worthiness. More simply, fear is what develops when we stop trusting in our own ability and start believing that external circumstances have the power to define or destroy us.

In earlier chapters, we learned that whatever we believe about ourselves will manifest. So during times of intense fear, it's important to remember who you thought you were before the disappointment…before the fear. Ask yourself, have you really changed that much? Does having a great job opportunity or a partner inherently make you a better or worse person? Once full of potential and promise, are you now somehow flawed and unworthy? Of course, the answer is *no*. The only thing that has changed is your focus. You went from being excited about your future to being fearful about your future. Chances are you never questioned your worthiness when you were in pursuit of what you wanted. You just expected good. You expected with certainty and great anticipation. This excited certainty is enthusiasm, and it is the arch enemy of fear.

> *Perspective*
>
> *On top of the hill,*
> *at the summit,*
> *there's Skill.*
> *But below,*
> *in the valley,*
> *there's Hope.*
> *-Kenya Jackson*

*****

enthusiasm

Enthusiasm is excited anticipation. It's zeal. It's fervor.

If you've ever been excited about something, then you probably remember the warm tingly waves rippling through your stomach. You can probably also remember how your smile felt as it slowly inflated your lips, and then spread across your face. Take a moment now to remember a time when you were excited about something. The anticipation of it kept you on a cloud of joy until moments after you received it. You were happy before you got it because you knew it was coming. You anticipated something good and therefore you felt good on the inside while you waited for it. It's the same feeling you had all those years while you were in school.

The unfortunate thing about this type of anticipation is that it's temporary. It's fleeting and it passes shortly after it appears. Chances are, once you got what you wanted you almost immediately stopped focusing on your ability to attract more good things to you. Indeed, after receiving something wanted most people just return to their default emotion— passive anticipation of bad things, with the occasional good thing on the side. Some people even start looking for something bad, immediately following something good. It's like they can't believe that things are actually going well for them, so they actively seek negativity.

The scenario I described above is tragic, and I am sure none of us wants to keep repeating it. So we have to make a choice. Instead of living in a state of complacent acceptance for all the "bads" in life, we must live every day like we're expecting good things to happen. Making a choice like this may seem easier said than done. But, I guess that depends on what you classify as easy.

We make plenty of agreements in this life. One of which is to agree that life is hard, unfair and so on. Isn't that a choice? Couldn't we choose to believe something else and therefore expect a different result? It's obvious that we can, because, as illustrated above, we do it in certain moments. Even on the worst of days and in the most challenging of circumstances, there are some things that can always bring us back to a happy place. The trick is to learn where that happy place comes from and channel it into your daily life. Enthusiasm can be your medium to do that.

building confidence

A few years ago, I consulted a psychologist about a fear of flying that had developed three years prior. I was surprised when he told me that my new fear of flying was really the result of a lack of confidence and a decrease in enthusiasm. In college, I held a regional office for my sorority. The position required me to travel. For more than two years, I zigzagged all across the region, nearly every weekend, with no issue. I would pray, and then fall asleep, most times staying asleep until I could feel the plane descending. Then one day, while on a connecting flight from Fort Lauderdale to Atlanta, all that changed.

It was a huge plane, one of the kinds with three rows. During meal service, the turbulence was so bad that the pilot suspended it, and asked the flight attendants to sit down. Children were screaming, people were praying, and I was just scared to death. I thought about never seeing my family again. Plus, in the back of my mind I knew that when I got off of this plane I would have to get on another. In the end, everything turned out okay. The turbulence was bad but brief, and my next flight was seamless. In fact, pretty much every flight I have been on since then has been seamless. What hasn't changed, however, is the immobilizing fear I feel whenever I buy a plane ticket or even think about a flight since then. In truth, after that flight, I lost all interest in traveling.

I was so surprised when my psychologist suggested that I was afraid because I had stopped being excited. Bear with me as I explain. He reasoned that I hadn't been afraid before because I knew there was a speaking engagement, or a conference on the other end of the runway. It was my anticipation of being needed that kept me from thinking something bad could happen. I knew that I had to be where I was going, and I was excited to be there.

But once my term ended and I was traveling for pleasure or familial obligation, I didn't feel as secure. My insecurity manifested itself as a heightened expectation that something bad would happen.

After some reflection, I was able to see his point. I realized that I had internalized my flight experiences. In some weird way, every time I had a great flight, my confidence increased. I felt safe and secure, expecting that this time would be no different than the last. Beyond that, my position made me feel worthy of safety. I knew that people were waiting for me wherever I was going. In the spirit of attachment, I had personalized the whole thing. It followed that when I had the bad flight, I interpreted it as a sign of personal inadequacy. The fear only increased when I was no longer in office. In my head, I reasoned that if something so terrible could happen to me when there were people waiting for me, what would happen once there weren't? I would fall out of the sky—that's what!

Luckily, I wasn't ready to accept that the only thing that made me worthy of life was a job. Furthermore, what surprised me was how many successful, seamless flights I had, yet how prominent the one bad flight had become in my mind. I had to admit, the whole thing was pretty silly!

Admittedly, the battle to overcome my fear of flying is far from behind me. However, I am more than grateful to know where it's coming from. In addition, I now know that sometimes, overcoming a fear is found in the determined fortitude needed to face it time and time again.

Remember, just as we learned not to trust ourselves, we can learn to trust ourselves again. All we have to do is be strong enough to face what threatens us and our confidence will grow. So, while I can't say my hands don't shake and my stomach doesn't drop every time I get on a plane, I make it a point to get excited about the journey and, most importantly, I get on the plane anyway.

You would think that after confronting something as scary as a fear of flying, I would be free from all the other fears I had accumulated over the years, or at least better equipped to deal with them. But I wasn't. Even after facing this particular fear repeatedly, it took years for me to extract and confront the true origin of my fear. When I did, I realized that fear had not only held captive my desire for happiness, it was also threatening to rob me of my self-esteem and my talent.

you're fired! (again): the erosion of my confidence

For as long as I can remember, I've been a lover of words and writing. I wrote as a hobby, or as a release. I never saw writing as a career, though. Instead, I pursued a more traditional career path (a safer one). I was always a good student and had good grades through high school and college. By the time I was twenty-five, I had a master's degree, had worked for two prominent nonprofit organizations and the mayor of a major suburb in my hometown. At the time, everyone was always telling me how smart and talented I was. I believed them. I was excited.

However, when I moved to Atlanta, things started to change for the worse. While I had had the opportunity to work at a variety of very prestigious organizations, I never quite felt like I belonged in any of them. It didn't take long for them to feel the same way because between 2006 and 2010, I was fired four times.[10]

My internship with a small cancer organization had just ended when a friend of the family told me that there was an opening at a larger cancer organization, one of the largest. I had never worked for such a prestigious organization and was frightened at the thought of it. My new boss was an up and coming giant in the nonprofit world. She had worked for the

---

[10] I thought having four jobs in four years was a lot, but according to www.quarterlifecrisis.com, the average American job-hops eight times before the age of thirty-two.

largest nonprofits and had a remarkable knack for coming into an organization and making major waves in just a few short years. She was very clear that she wanted the same thing for me. Since the department was just me and her, I had to start out as an administrative assistant, but for the same reason my duties were pretty extensive.

She negotiated a healthy salary for me. I was making more money than my parents. I can remember getting my pay check and seeing a comma in between the four digits. I was so excited about all the money, that when my friends asked me about my new job I would often joke, "It's all about the comma."

Things went pretty well initially. My boss and I got along. She and I talked about a lot of things. One thing in particular that we spoke about often was how uncomfortable she was being the only director in the finance department that didn't have a finance degree. As a matter of fact, neither of us did, and we were the only two in the department that didn't. This tidbit of information didn't cause me much alarm. I kind of saw it as a good thing. I thought I must have been pretty awesome if they chose me without one. I tried to communicate the same thing to her, but the seeds of fear and insecurity had already been planted. It was too late. Her insecurity led her to be overly concerned about what the other directors said or thought, especially about me.

So, although she and I had agreed that I could come to work anytime between 9:00 a.m. and 9:30 a.m., when the other directors said she was being too lax on me, that time changed to 7:45 a.m. I won't lie—prior to the change, I definitely took my liberties, but it wasn't habitual. Soon I was required to come in early and leave late.

Eventually, she started to loan me out to other business units to organize files and do other administrative work. I was expected to complete all of our work as well as theirs. I was also expected to take the snide insults from the heads of other business units and behave as her lap dog. Obedient, quiet, and submissive. Offended doesn't even begin to describe how I felt about the situation. But I ate it, considering the money and the opportunity. It wasn't until a real opportunity presented itself that I realized that I had been bought and sold by her, and any deviation from her plan would be perceived as insubordinate.

In the fall of 2006, Merck Pharmaceuticals unveiled their new cervical cancer vaccine. There was quite a bit of controversy surrounding the vaccine, and I took it personally when we, the leading cancer organization in the world, hesitated to weigh in on the argument. This was our business. People were depending on us. We needed to say something. Soon.

As a victim of cancer loss, I acted right away. I contacted the Chief Operating Officer of the organization, and set up a meeting with her. I wanted to know what we were doing about cervical cancer, a 100 percent preventable cancer that was killing thousands of Black and Latino women every year.

In the end, my meeting was bittersweet. I was told (by her designee) that the bulk of money raised for cancer went to breast cancer research. As a result, cervical cancer was not on our radar as a priority just yet. In a few years, when it reached the forefront of the global cancer conversation, we would be more vocal on the matter. I guess until then, I was just supposed to return to my cubicle and alphabetize some files. To make matters worse, my boss thought I was out of line for setting up the meeting in the first place. My priority was to my department and to her. I was unsettled because I felt my larger priority was curing cancer, or preventing it at best. My uneasiness was perceived as defiance, and in less than week I was terminated.

The experience was so upsetting because I felt I had done the right thing by caring about curing cancer…but I was soon reminded by a coworker that if we found a cure to cancer, none of us would have a job. She was right. And my forgetting this fact had cost me my livelihood. It was best for me to stop rocking the boat and just shut my mouth.

I learned to be afraid.

For this reason, losing my job sent me into a dangerous spiral of blame and depression. I told myself that I had lost a good job. No, the best job I would ever have. I carried this shame for a year before I gained a part-time seasonal position with another large nonprofit. I was more successful at this job, but when the position expired, and I was not offered full-time employment, fear set in again.

Seven months passed.

I was behind on my rent and all my bills.

I was asking my friends, family, and sorority
sisters for money.

Desperate, I become a cocktail waitress at a popular adult
entertainment club. After the excitement of making $300–
$350 a night wore off, I could feel the fear building in my
belly again. Was this all I could do? Be a waitress? In a strip
club? Was I a failure? I frantically began to look for another
nine to five job.

In less than a month, I found a new job. It was another large
nonprofit. But this time, it was also a sexist, racist,
homophobic one. Still, I tried hard to fit in. Even when they
attacked everything, from my hair to my clothes. It wasn't
until months later that I was able to discern how the constant
psychological abuse I endured had eroded my self-image.
After months of not measuring up to an impossible standard
set forth by people who themselves had yet to meet it, I
started to interpret my failure at work as personal failure. I
believed that since I was a failure as a person, I was incapable
of being trusted to make any lasting life decisions for myself.
My confidence was destroyed.

I understand now that it was my attachment to my role as an
employee and my attachment to being successful in that role
that handicapped me. The overall functionality of the job was
not to secure me personally. It was a means to an end. A job
did not have the power to make me feel whole, smart,
independent or any other good-feeling adjective. The job was

76

not me. Besides, how could I love and value myself and choose to stay in a situation that was so uncomfortable? The answer was simple. Fear. I was so afraid of being perceived as a failure that I did not care what I had to go through to prove that I wasn't. I blamed myself. I had created my situation and I didn't trust myself to make a decision to stay or go. So, I just endured it until the Universe manifested my subconscious thoughts and freed me from the situation. I then took the rejection as validation that I had ruined another perfect opportunity. If I couldn't make the next opportunity work, I was surely a failure (of course I couldn't, because I kept getting fired).

Every time I got fired, it eroded more and more of my confidence. I couldn't be excited about anything, not even my next job, because I was so fearful that I would say or do something to ruin it. The only thing that felt even remotely positive about all this was that being unemployed four times in four years left plenty of time for introspection and soul searching. Eventually, I started to uncover some shadow beliefs about myself.

I remembered that one of my close family members had always told me what a horrible work ethic I had. She would commonly tell me that I was lazy and that I never wanted to work. Her words had major implications on the way I felt about myself. They made me angry with myself. So angry, that I used her words to fuel *new* feelings of unworthiness. In my last two jobs before writing this book, I actually accumulated so much fear, blame, and guilt about my worthiness that I became physically ill.

Moreover, losing the jobs only fortified the ideas I had internalized about being lazy and having a poor work ethic. I dismissed the time in my life when I worked from seven o'clock in the morning until four o'clock in the evening, only to put in another six hours at my night job. I also ignored the entire year that I spent working ten to twelve hours a day as a waitress in the airport. None of these things were enough to convince me that I was worthy of success. Here, I pause to remind you about our conversation concerning mental schemas. Remember, once a schema is formed, ideas that contradict it are ignored.

The day I got fired from my last job, I called my best friends. I asked them, as I always did when I lost a job—what is wrong with me? The answer they gave me this time was different. They asked why I kept doing this to myself. Why did I keep trying to do something that had never felt natural? Why wouldn't I embrace the opportunity of the empty. S P A C E I was in? Furthermore, why didn't I trust myself to do what I had always loved?

They told me that what was wrong with me had nothing to do with losing jobs. This was about attachment and fear. I had never been happy at work and I had never expected to be. I had also become attached to the predictable outcome of being a failure at work. So when it happened, I wasn't surprised.

Mistakenly, I didn't see my lack of happiness as an indicator that I may be pursuing career paths that were not a good fit for me. This was a mistake because happiness is one of the most powerful indicators that we are in alignment with source energy. Therefore, if something makes us miserable, it is perfectly okay for us to stop doing it. It occurred to me that I had never been happy at work because I was chasing the predicable instead of chasing my passion.

If I were honest with myself, I would have to admit that the only reason I had been interested in working any of the jobs was because of how (I thought) it made me appear to other people. I felt like having a big important job showed my ability to make good safe decisions. The money was proof that I wasn't worthless, and the title was proof that I wasn't a failure. But perhaps I had it all wrong. Perhaps I was better suited to pursue my passion of being a writer. Perhaps I would be successful doing something that actually felt good.

Then suddenly, like a ton of bricks, it hit me and I realized, I was even more scared of doing what *may* feel good, than I was of doing what I *knew* felt bad.

Throughout my life there was always one thing that I had— words. When life disappointed me, I could always go back and read the poems or short stories that I had previously written, and laugh and smile and cry. I could always find a poem to illustrate how I was feeling. I loved it. It was mine.

In fact, in 2006, I wrote a book of poetry called *Private Protest*. I am looking at it in its original white binder as I write this. I never shared it because I loved it and I was terrified to let anything ruin it for me. What if publishing my writing opened me up to criticism? What if people hated it? What if I really was lazy and just needed to pray for some discipline and focus? What if this writing thing was all some pipe dream, better left as a "what if"?

On a deeper level, these shadow beliefs were probably causing the lack of success. I was afraid to be the person I wanted to be, the person the Universe had been setting me up to be since I was a child. The person that died the day I got fired from my first job.

It was the fear that needed to be terminated, the fear that needed to be evicted. So I sought to replace it. I knew how fear had manifested itself in my life. What I didn't know was what would happen if I fearlessly proceeded in the direction of joy without it. I got excited and I realized it was impossible to be excited and fearful at the same time. The fear wasn't big enough to squash the enthusiasm.

I started to meditate on the Tao Te Ching[11] in the morning. I wrote snippets of poetry on my Twitter page, and posted cool statuses on my Facebook page like "going to play in S P A C E" or "lost in S P A C E."

I started to embrace the artistry, creativity, and honesty that came so natural to me. Sometimes, I would sit on my bed and let the sun shine on my naked legs as I wrote. Other times, I'd play my favorite songs and type all day.

---

[11] The Tao Te Ching is a philosophical text written by Lao Tze. The specific date it was written is unclear, but it is believed to be centuries old.

On my twenty-seventh birthday, I got the word $S P A C E$, tattooed on my arm, and started to write this book. That same year I started a blog and began posting videos on YouTube. A year after that, I entered my first book contest. And a year after that I started lining up motivational speaking gigs. I felt amazing. Once I discovered the empty. $S P A C E$ of my situation, I stopped being scared and I stared being enthusiastic.

I now recognized that none of this would have happened had I not lost that first job. Loosing that job gave me both the time and the motivation to seek happiness outside of traditional employment. In hindsight, it's one of the best things that ever happened to me.

Every day, I make a conscious effort to be excited about life and all the wonderful things that are happening *right now*. I have resolved to continue to expect good, even when all I see around me seems bad. I had no issue doing it the other way around, so I don't see the harm in choosing to believe that life is fair, people are good, and things work out. Besides, writing this book is the most important thing I have ever done, and I am excited to share the *best* of me with the world. I hope that it will bring out the *best* of you. I have no clue how many copies this book will sell, but I am typing each word with love, with purpose, and with joy. I've made a decision to shift my orientation from fear to enthusiasm.

On the vision board that hangs in my living room, I cut out the words, "I will participate today." These words are a constant reminder to me that no matter what is happening in my life, I will not give up on myself. I truly believe that this human experience is a cosmic dance between our human selves and our spirit selves. Our spirit selves will give us whatever it is that we want. If we seek abundance, the Universe is waiting to give to us, but we have to show up. We have to participate, even if we are scared out of our wits!

Today, I replace my fear with enthusiasm.

Note to self
(and everybody else):
On Fear

I expect and prepare for the best. I trust
that the Universe is working with me to
bring good into my life every day.

I am the optimistic S P A C E of
Enthusiasm.

Chapter 4

S P A C E from Destruction:
S P A C E in Creation

From the time I was a very small child, I have loved words. I loved to read words, to spell words, and to repeat the "grown-up" words I heard my mom whisper or spell to my aunt. I relished copying those particular words in my notebook and drawing rainbows and hearts around them. I thought my "adult word" pictures were funny—my mom, not so much.

My love affair with words started early on and has only continued to grow over the years. Even now, I research the definitions and derivations of my favorite words. I am always ever so careful to construct my sentences, poems, and conversations deliberately and with respect. In fact, my love for the word S P A C E created the idea and framework for this book. Yes, I love words.

As a result, I am aware of the many ways that we abuse both the power and purpose of words. Just think about it. As children we learned that "Sticks and stones may break my bones…but words will never hurt me." I don't know about you, but in my life, words have done far more damage than any stick or stone has. If the children at my elementary school had been caught throwing sticks and stones at me, they would have been suspended or disciplined immediately. Yet, there were countless times when quiet insults and verbal attacks went completely unnoticed and unpunished. Even when these attacks were reported, the response was always the same. One person denies, while the other insists. It's classic and ironic— my word against theirs!

It's no surprise then that when I started to collect my thoughts for this chapter, I felt words would be the best place to begin. Why? Because words are the most basic manifestations of our thoughts. We say what we think. If we are destructive in our speech, chances are we are having equally destructive thoughts.

Interestingly, we may not always be able to identify when we are being destructive. We are so accustomed to gossiping or telling little white lies that we think destructive speech is normal. Be careful here though because, just because an act is common, it doesn't make it natural. And just because an act is accepted, it doesn't make it any less destructive.

The Noble Eightfold Path of Buddhism has strict rules regarding how we should speak to each other. The principle of "right speech" holds that humans should abstain from false speech, slanderous speech, and from using harsh words. It also says that we should abstain from idle chatter that lacks purpose or depth. Positively phrased, this means we should tell the truth, speak friendly, warmly, and gently, and only when necessary.[12]

---

[12] http://www.thebigview.com/buddhism/eightfoldpath.html

I'm sure many would also agree that praying, chanting, and singing are linguistic pipelines to a higher power. The Bible and other sacred texts oftentimes entreat followers to "ask and it shall be given," or to profess our love for God. How then, do we rationalize that our prayerful words have power, but our destructive words do not?

Impossible.

While there are many ways that we destroy ourselves and each other with our words, there are three types of destructive words that seem to be most common: (1) angry words, (2) judging words or gossip, and (3) false words or lies. Let's examine angry words and judging words more closely.

Some time ago, in my Buddhist meditation group, the teacher spoke to us about anger. He said anger was a dangerous state of mind because an angry mind has the intention to destroy.

Many times when we are angry our knee-jerk reaction is to say something destructive, something harmful. This is especially true when things don't go the way we planned (or people don't behave the way we think they should). Maybe a loved one disappoints us, or the traffic is congested. Perhaps we had a late night and an early morning. At times like this, it's easy to have an unconscious reaction and lash out. We see our lashing out as justified and ignore the karmic cycle we have just initiated by abusing the gift of expression.

The Universe is not in the business of distinguishing between good and bad, right and wrong. The Universe applies the same rules to every situation—its one law, the law of symmetry and continuity. If our prayerful words are powerful and have the strength to create and manifest good in our lives, we must accept that our destructive words have some power as well. One couldn't exist without the other.

Remember that, the next time you opt to go-off on, lie to, or talk about someone else. No matter the circumstance, your words have power and possibility.

what you see...is what you feel...is what you get

At first, it was just the news that I had to avoid, but lately there seems to be an overall obsession with destruction and death, permeating every facet of our mainstream media. Then, with the onset of television shows like *CSI*, where they dissect the entrails of human beings as if they're the fetal pigs of an eleventh grade biology lab, you almost need to avoid television altogether.

A few years ago, I started calling these types of television programs, "death, murder, kill." For the life of me, I can't understand what is even remotely appealing about watching someone get murdered, raped, or victimized.

Now, I am sure that the writers of the "death, murder, kill" conglomerate are not attempting to poison our minds with images of doom. They are simply "giving the people what they want." The sad part is—we do want it.

Nowadays, fictional television shows that glorify violence and rape are being rivaled by their reality counterparts. It's not uncommon for reality TV shows to place people of opposing walks of life under the same roof, just to hear the insults fly and watch the proverbial shit hit the fan. Then, at the show's end, there is supposed to be some magical catharsis that takes place to get the human experiments to realize how their actions can and have impacted other people. They promise to change, until the next season—or the next episode.

At the risk of sounding like a hippie, utopian, one-worlder…I just don't get it. I don't like it. I don't like seeing people suffer or die or get hit. It's just not funny to me. Pain is real, and when the cameras are off, how do these real people recover from the effects of being exposed and exploited?

The supposition and underlying message is that, in order to get ahead or be successful, one must destroy another person. Merit is almost never a true factor as much as it is a hindrance.

Next to work, entertainment is what we spend the majority of our time on. And since work is what we have to do and entertainment is what we choose to do, it can be a strong indicator of our personality.

Oscar Wilde said, "Life imitates art" and metaphysical law says, "You are what you think about." Since our senses give context and meaning to our experiences, and our experiences reinforce our expectations, then our senses have a key role in shaping our lives. So, if destruction is what we see, hear, and talk about, it will ultimately become our life experience.

Having had such little experience with the fullness and immortality of our real selves, things, people, and situations are more familiar when they are broken or negative. A mirror for our true feelings about ourselves, broken experiences are predictable and, in some sense, safe. Consequently, feeding our psyche negative images can indirectly cause us to become fractured little people with low expectations.

We say things like, "this is too good to be true" or "all that glitters is not gold," as if we want to constantly reinforce a spirit of lack and fear. What we are really saying is that we will never be happy, whole, or fulfilled, because we are not worth it.

In keeping with this, let's examine our feelings surrounding graduate school entrance exams, the LSAT or GMAT, in particular. Oftentimes, before we even take the test, we tell ourselves that no one gets a good score on the first try. Subconsciously, we decide that the test is hard and that we will likely have to take it more than once. We then flood our consciousness with images of failure and difficulty by reading all the scary stories about how many people fail on their first try.

In the meantime, we continue to study diligently. We may even take online courses and get a tutor. We convince ourselves that we're ready for the test, pretending that we haven't already decided the outcome of the situation. Then when we fail, we're disappointed but not surprised. We take the test the second time and do much better and ta-dah, we were right.

Psychology calls this phenomenon **the self-fulfilling prophecy.** Unlike a traditional prophecy, one that objectively uses the facts of a situation to draw a conclusion, the self-fulfilling prophecy is a predication that we make true.[13] Denotatively, the self-fulfilling prophecy directly or indirectly causes itself to become true, by the very terms of the prophecy itself. In other words, we do what we said we were going to do, simply because we said we were going to do it, only on a subconscious level.

If we inundate our minds with certain images or ideas, our minds will begin to make predictions on future outcomes based on what we have fed it in the past. That's why it is of the utmost importance that we think twice before flooding ourselves with any type of negativity, be it what we watch or what we choose to believe.

Going back to our TV example, it doesn't matter whether you want to create more death and destruction in your own life at all. What matters is the fact that our mind begins to see these awful things as possible. In order for the possibility to make sense at all, we have to be able to identify with the possibility in some way. So the fact that "people" get raped and

---

[13] David G. Myers. *Social Psychology*. 7th ed. (Columbus, Ohio: McGraw-Hill Higher Education, 2002.)

murdered, on some level means that we *could* get raped and murdered. Make sense?

*****

creation

In high school, a friend of mine had a sticker on her binder that read, "The opposite of war is not peace; it's creation." At sixteen, I was intrigued, not only by the play on words but by the overall concept. I loved the idea of creation being the antithesis of destruction. I liked it because I could see this relationship working in every circumstance. Most people, when they contemplate destruction, are thinking only of war. So the natural assumption is that peace is the opposite. However, what happens when the destruction isn't related to a definitive war? Peace doesn't offer complete transcendence in these cases.

Luckily, most of us will never have a face-to-face encounter with war proper, but we will all experience destructive people, circumstances and attitudes. Creation can be a means to transform each.

belief and expectation

Everything in the world started out as an idea. Ev-er-y-thing! According to the Bible, the world itself was formed from an intention to create. So, when I have my moments of doubt and fear, I remind myself that if an idea created the cosmos, my ideas, like my words, have power and possibility.

Creating the life we want is a process. It is something that takes both knowledge and practice to execute properly. Let's take a moment to look at the creative process as it relates to belief and expectation.

A host of popular metaphysicists contend that the creative process starts with an intention or a desire to create. I am going to disagree slightly and say that the creative process starts with belief. In truth, it's impossible for us to intend a certain thing to happen if we don't believe it can happen. This is not to say that we can't call things into existence without knowing how they will come to pass. The *knowing how* part is less important than the *believing it can* part.

I am willing to argue that, at thirteen years old, you had no clue how to drive, but you knew that you wanted to. Furthermore, you knew you could because of what you had observed in the past. Now, here is where the belief issue gets sticky. You will notice that part of the reason why you believed you could do a certain thing was because of what you had observed (heard, or read about, etc.). This trips some people up because they base their beliefs (and subsequent intentions) only on what they have seen or experienced. This is a mistake.

Yes, belief is necessary for intention, and intention is necessary for creation, but observation is not necessary for belief. If observation were necessary for belief, then the only things we would be able to create would be those things that have already been created. And since no human is omniscient, and none of us has seen all there is to see, we would all be fundamentally unable to create anything new. Of course, we know that this is not the case either.

We are left with the question, *how do I create something new when I have never seen it?* The answer is relatively simple: we find encouragement in the same idea that led us to be destructive—possibility. We agree that anything is possible, both seen and unseen.

Taking this one step further, we agree that:

Good is possible *for me.* [14]
Happiness is possible *for me.*
Fulfillment is possible *for me.*

If this is our anchor belief, all of our other beliefs will fall in line with it. You will notice that the "for me" part is just as important as the possibility. It's important because as we observe the success of others, our attached, judgmental, and fearful ego may try to persuade us that while good is possible…it isn't possible for us. But just as you included yourself in the possibility for bad, you must also include yourself in the possibility for good.

Okay, so now that we have addressed our beliefs, we can formulate our intentions. Once the intentions are formed, our subconscious mind, or spirit, begins to bring our intentions to us in the form of tangible things. There is an entire science (The Law of Attraction) dedicated to this process, but here it

---

[14] I call this the "master affirmation," because it works in every situation.

is only important to understand the importance of beliefs and intention. Once we know the importance of our beliefs, and that those beliefs are chiefly fed by what we observe, the process of choosing what to observe becomes all the more important.

Take a moment to ponder what you watch on television, listen to on the radio, read about, or discuss with your friends. How is your participation in these activities or conversations helping to create the life you want?

When I was faced with this question, I was saddened by the answer because, for me, destruction had become an addiction. I, like many people, craved the dismal predictability that it provided and was lost without it.

In the preceding chapter, we discovered that there is an overarching belief that life is hard, a bitch, and so on. This belief was presented as a founding principle of fear. In this case, fear served as a coping mechanism. A **coping mechanism**[15] is a stress management tool. Fear helps us to cope with stress by protecting us from being disappointed when things don't go our way.

By the same token, destruction is also a coping mechanism— a defense mechanism, specifically. **Defense mechanisms** also help us to manage stress, but oftentimes they do so by unconsciously distorting reality.[16] So, when we are

---

[15] Changing Minds. "Coping Mechanisms" Accessed on January 4, 2013
http://changingminds.org/explanations/behaviors/coping/coping.htm.
[16] R.J. Comer, *Abnormal Psychology.* 4th ed. New York: Worth Publishing, 2002.

destructive toward others, we *think* we are guarding ourselves against ideas and people that have the power to harm us. We rationalize that we will get them before they get us. What we are really saying is that people are out to get me, or I have an enemy. This type of defense mechanism is called **projection.** [17] It's the essence of "you make me so mad." We want to blame our anger on someone else instead of taking responsibility for our own feelings and emotions. Projecting is problematic because it actually makes us more susceptible to being abused, taken advantage of, and so on. Plus, we get what we expect, so if we think we have an enemy or an army of haters…we will attract one. Then when we do, we will use our experience as ammunition and validation to be destructive toward others. Thus the cycle continues.

self-destruction

Destructive behavior is not always directed toward other people. **Self-destruction** is a primary means of coping with stress for many people. Modern psychology cites self-destruction as a "means by which we externalize internal feelings of stress, fear, and pain." As we are having these feelings on the inside, our mind seeks an outlet, so we hurt ourselves. Something in us wants to see the pain. Alcoholism, drug abuse, and sexual promiscuity are just a few of the ways we as humans seek to hurt ourselves.

Whenever we are using a defense mechanism of any kind, it is because we are unable to address our situation in a healthy

---

[17] Susan K. Whitborne, "The Essential Guide to Defense Mechanisms." Psychology Today. (2011) 2.

way. Instead, we choose to cope or "just get through" the situation by using drugs, alcohol, sex, anger, etc. Of course, when we are feeling the unpleasant feelings, "getting through" seems good enough. However, if we fail to extract the root of the problem (our thoughts, beliefs, and expectations), it is likely to resurface time and time again. Then what? More destruction.

When I was in college, my friends and I were members of a service organization that mentored young girls. We selected ten girls, each with their own set of social and academic challenges. As a psychology student, my role was to work one-on-one with the behavioral problems of each girl.

Before the program began, the guidance counselor at the school warned me that one of the young ladies in the program was dealing with a particularly sensitive issue. She was a cutter. She had been the victim of sexual abuse and had since been diagnosed with a laundry list of emotional and psychological disorders. Since the abuse and subsequent diagnosis, she had also become increasingly promiscuous. She would have sex with anyone who showed even a modicum of interest in her, just because, "they seemed to like it."

The cutting had started after kids at the school found out about her "extracurricular activities." Feeling alone, victimized, and now marginalized, she felt powerless to defend herself against her attackers. So she took her pain out on the one person she knew she could overpower: herself. I could tell that the guidance counselor thought she was crazy, but I thought she was remarkable.

When I met her, next to her smile, the tiny keloids decorating her wrists were her most endearing feature. It was impossible not to notice them, but that is what I loved about them. As my eyes, and eventually fingers, skimmed the raised bruises, I could not help but see the miracle of healing. Yes, she was scarred. And, yes, she had done it to herself, but she had also allowed herself to heal. Now, when she looked at her arms she was constantly reminded of how she had been victorious over something in her life.

I thought about the other young ladies in the program and even the young women who were helping to run the program. I thought of all the times our emotional pain surfaced, and the many ways we chose to deal with it. Not nearly as brave as she was, we chose to cope by drinking, or smoking, or overeating. We hid our pain and our destructive behavior beneath the façade of normalcy.

But there was no way that this young lady could hide her pain. She wore it on her wrists, her arms, her thighs. And to me, that took courage—courage that I had yet to find within myself.

Having hidden my addiction for more than ten years at that time, I internalized my experience with her. I knew that shame had kept me from being honest about how I was handling the pain surrounding my mother's death. I wasn't a cutter, but I picked myself incessantly. I would sit for hours and pick at the skin on the bottom of my feet, sometimes until they bled or became hard for me to walk on. I bit my nails and nipped at the skin surrounding them. I stood in the mirror and picked at my face, creating black marks and scars. And I neurotically played with my hair, until I was practically bald in one spot. I was being self-destructive too, and no one noticed. Even now it's hard to write about my addiction, because I am aware that many people still don't know the extent of it. Yet in the spirit of that young girl who touched me so deeply years ago, I am ready to be honest about it now.

addicted

I was twelve years old the first time my best friend and I sat in the narrow space between the wall and my chest of drawers to inhale the intoxicating smell of Pine Sol. It seemed normal, like a natural progression after years of sniffing white-out and permanent markers. Everyone took deep breaths as gas was being pumped, right? Well, even if everyone didn't, she and I did and that made it okay. Tanya[18] was my closest friend. She and I did everything together, including this. I didn't feel guilty or weird about it at all. Even when the Pine Sol bottle became a hidden treasure that I fanaticized about uncovering at the end of each day, or when I began to notice that the slight burn of the cleanser paled in comparison to the faster, quicker burn that I could achieve if I sniffed rubbing alcohol (both less inviting than the capful of shoe polish). Through it all, the idea of addiction never occurred to me.

---

[18] Names have been changed to protect privacy.

I did a little research and discovered that there was one particular ingredient in all of the substances that I liked to sniff. It was called alcohol denat, the active ingredient in rubbing alcohol, a variety of body sprays, nail polish remover, astringent, and hand sanitizer. Each of these I kept hidden among the lotions in my closest, in plain sight yet completely unnoticed—just like my addiction. The body spray made me sleepy. The nail polish remover and astringent gave me headaches. The hand sanitizer stung my nose and burned my nostrils numb. Each brought an instantaneous relaxation. It didn't feel like being high, but it was something that I couldn't live without.

Soon twelve became thirteen, thirteen became fifteen, fifteen became twenty, twenty became twenty-five, twenty-five became twenty-eight…and as each year passed, I buried my secret even deeper.

I resolved that no one could smell the solvent on my upper lip or detect the circular rash around my nose and mouth. I had learned to blame my short-term memory loss on being busy or having "a lot going on" in my life. The speech impediment and slurred speech I just ignored altogether. From time to time, I'd do an Internet search on the effects of huffing, but I never took the results seriously. It wasn't glue. I wasn't drooling. Most importantly, I wasn't an addict.

In the summer of 2005, I met the woman of my dreams. She was beautiful, smart, understanding and gentle. I loved her almost instantly, and there were moments that her love for me was the only thing that reminded me of my humanity. I had struggled with depression my whole life, a depression that oftentimes made me feel alone and marginalized, but she made me feel plugged in. I trusted her, and eventually I told her.

Cautiously, I explained the half-empty bottles of household cleanser strewn about the house, and the reason I couldn't spend nights at her house without stopping at mine for just five minutes. I let the truth roll from my lips like toilet paper, unrolling layer after layer of secrecy and shame. I knew she would be soft, and I knew she would understand. Her response was twofold: empathy and intolerance. Some people may think the two can't coexist, but indeed they can. It was as if she said, "I understand why you thought you had to do what you did, but you can't continue to do it, at least not with me in your life."

Confident that I wasn't an addict, I assumed quitting wouldn't be a problem, so I agreed to do it. I told myself that I just liked the way the stuff smelled. That's it. I didn't get high from it, there was no ulterior motive. Then I tried to quit and started to lie.

When I didn't huff, I was irritable. I was on edge and always ready to argue. So, I evaded my girlfriend's questions about the "last time" with ease and skill. I hadn't quit, and I didn't plan to. What was the big deal anyway? It wasn't that big of a deal at all.

In the fall of 2007, just after our two-year anniversary and subsequent engagement, my wife-to-be told me that the

101

mother of her children could not and would not be an addict. In a last ditch attempt to save my relationship, I found myself in a roomful of what I deemed "real" addicts at a Narcotics Anonymous meeting. I was embarrassed. During the meeting, one of the participants stood up and said she had a burning desire to do her drug of choice in that moment. When someone said that, the entire meeting had to stop, and we all had to focus our attention and energy on that person.

The lady was crying. She said it wasn't that she had a hard time not doing the drug; her issue had to do with her desire for the drug. She said it was easy to just not do it, but in her heart and mind, she couldn't find a reason not to do it. She said her life didn't matter to her anymore; she didn't care if she died. Her children had been taken away from her because of the addiction, so she knew they would be taken care of if something happened to her.

Why should she care if she lived or died? Could her quality of life really diminish anymore?

Didn't she deserve some joy in the days that she had left, even if that joy came as a by-product of the very drug that had swallowed her entire life?

Her words struck me. I felt like she was giving a voice to the hopelessness that so many addicts feel. I could totally understand what she was saying, because I felt that same way. It wasn't that I couldn't stop huffing, I absolutely could. I didn't want to. I liked it. And I didn't care what it was costing me. I was willing to pay the cost if it meant I could have my addiction, my moments of drowsy peace, my secret stress reliever.

Huffing and picking were how I dealt with things. How I defended myself from all that was attacking my mind on a daily basis. When I had a stressful day, or a fight with a loved one, I rushed home to peel the skin from my feet and inhale the burning relaxation of my comfort. If I stopped, who would take care of me? How would I take the edge off? It wasn't worth it to me. I needed it. And it wasn't fair that I was being forced to give it up.

I was interested, however, in why I needed it. Around the same time that all this was going on, I started to notice that I was increasingly angry. I had road rage to the point of tears and would throw things at my girlfriend frequently. I started to see a therapist, and she told me that I was dealing with a mild case of anxiety. The picking was a symptom (I didn't bother to mention the huffing). But I knew the two went hand-in-hand, because I never got as much satisfaction doing one without the other.

Once I began to link huffing and anxiety, I felt I was getting somewhere. Not far enough to quit, but far enough to pay attention to when and why I was destroying myself. I became aware of how nervous I was, especially in certain situations. Namely, work. The previous two years (2006–2008) had been beyond stressful. I went from being the youngest person in the office with a boss who treated me like a peon, to being unemployed for almost a year and becoming 100 percent dependent on my girlfriend.

In the midst of all of this, I was also a full-time graduate student. I was confused, angry, overcommitted, overweight, and sad. I had a hard time merging my feelings of inadequacy with all the great expectations that everyone had for me. There was so much pressure, so many people counting on me to do or be something. They had no clue that I was suffocating beneath it all.

I traced the negative feelings back sixteen years, to the weeks and months right after my mother's death. I could remember how much everyone loved her. How highly they all spoke of her. How much she meant to my aunt, her only sibling—and to my cousin, her only niece. She had meant so much to so many, and suddenly, after a two-year battle with cancer, she was gone. All that was left of her was me, and I was expected to be the keeper of every hope and dream they ever had for her.

No one was prepared for the loss—let alone for dealing with the unruly twelve year old she left behind. My aunt and cousin weren't even able to talk to me about my mother for years after her death. I learned that any unresolved feelings about my mother would need to be buried deep beneath a polished exterior. I would need to be strong for my aunt, the way my mother had been strong for the family before she died.

I watched my cousin, only twenty-five at the time, work three jobs and go to school, in an effort to support me without using the insurance money my mom had left me. I watched my aunt pack on pound after pound, eating her pain. Neither of them shed a tear, instead they just did what they had to do. I respected them and I wanted to do my part. My being sad only increased the stress and pain that they felt. I knew they were working so hard because they wanted me to be happy. How could I be so ungrateful as to be sad? Crying about my mother's death wasn't going to bring her back. It was best that I just move on with my life.

At twelve years old, moving on meant repressing my pain. My mother had died of cancer, so there was no one to blame. And there was no one for me to talk to about it. So, I learned to hide it, to place it neatly in the bottom of my rubbing-alcohol bottle, each whiff burying my mother's memory deeper and deeper. It worked. I wasn't sad, at least not that anyone could see. To the world, I was a well-adjusted, well-rounded, healthy teenager...and young adult. No one ever assumed that I was hiding such a dangerous secret, and even when my family did find out about what was going on, they never knew the extent of it. I had been successful at hiding my addiction and pain for over half my life.

Until one Monday night.

Intervention

On Monday nights my roommate and I watch *Intervention*. It's a show about addicts and the people who love them. The people who love the addict are interested in helping them, so they bombard the person with love letters and an ultimatum. It's a tough-love type of thing. They tell the addict, "Get treatment or else." It was midnight, and I was alone, and so high from sniffing my body spray that my eyes were barely open. I was sleepy and had a headache from the fumes…when the tears began to roll.

There would be no intervention for me, because no one knew. I had hidden my addiction beneath my degrees, beneath my executive career, beneath my smile and the chronic depression which warranted my being alone and groggy looking all the time. I had hidden it in the pages of my poetry, where my clandestine confessions blended in with the meter and rhyme of the verse. I was an addict just like the ones on television. I was shrouded in shame and had no recollection of my life before huffing. I had done it my whole life and concealed it my whole life too.

I had been successfully destroying myself without anyone noticing for more than sixteen years. No scars on my arms. No catalog of suitors waiting to publish accounts of my sexual prowess. No empty alcohol bottles beneath my bed. No inconspicuous weight problem. To the naked eye, there was nothing. Only I knew the truth of what had been eating me for so long.

So, here's the inconvenient truth, the one I had been so unwilling to face. Since most of us work just as hard trying to hide our destruction as we do actually destroying ourselves, there may not be an intervention for you either. Your family and friends may not rush into your room and pry the razor from your hand. Your partner may not think to pour all the alcohol in the house down the drain one day. Your siblings may not see your messy house and disheveled hair as a cry for help. It's not that no one cares; it's just that life is happening to all of us at the same time, and we are all equally ill-equipped to deal with it. If you need help, reach out. Someone is waiting to listen.

The second inconvenient truth is that, more often than not, our self-destructive behavior is the result of unresolved pain. Quite honestly, there are no quick fixes when it comes to healing pain. The only way to heal is to experience it—fully. Cry. Scream. Hit something. Curse. Do what you have to do to get the emotion out of you, and then do the work you need to do to mentally and emotionally recover. The people who are telling you to be strong are wrong. You don't have to be strong. You can feel what you are feeling. You are not wrong for being in pain. When someone dies, it hurts. When a relationship ends, it hurts. When bad things happen, it hurts. It's okay to be sad and to be angry. It is also okay to give yourself permission to grieve and mourn. The reality is, if you don't allow yourself to experience the emotions, they will manifest themselves in another way. Usually in a way that is destructive.

Our bodies and spirits all exist in perfect balance. Because all anger is rooted in pain, the fact that you're angry enough with yourself to do something to hurt yourself only means that you're hurting. So, deal with your pain in a real way. Don't be afraid of it. Pain can't hurt you. It can't destroy you. Only you can destroy you.

I had carried the pain of losing my mother for my whole life and had secretly blamed myself for what happened. I felt like I wasn't there for her when she died. I felt like I never told her how much I loved her. At ten, I couldn't deal with watching my mother wither away in front of me, her body frail, dark, and bald because of the chemo. Her attitude short and volatile, because of the steroids. My family broken and compromised upon losing its matriarch.

I retreated, and, by the time I came to, she was in a hospital, dying. As much as I wanted to be there for her, I couldn't. I was too young and just didn't understand what was happening. For all the years that followed her death, I made it my mission to absolve myself of this sin by punishing myself daily for what I hadn't done for her. I didn't think I deserved to be happy. I couldn't hurt myself enough. The huffing became my purging process, gently ushering me into a cloudy haze of indifference. I didn't want to care. I just wanted to be sleepy. Numb.

The crazy thing was the more I retreated into myself, the stronger I appeared to everyone else.

On the outside looking in, people saw a strong survivor—someone who had not only lived through something terrible, but had overcome it. As a result, I became the go-to person for all of my friends. I was the resident psychologist to countless people at a very young age. So much so, that I chose psychology as my career path. I think I was comfortable in this role because it gave me some authority—some strength. In helping other people, I didn't have to focus on my own problems, and it only fortified the persona I was trying to portray. No one would ever suspect that their therapist or best friend was a depressed, self-destructive drug addict.

Over time, I've learned that people sometimes make the mistake of believing that, just because someone has lived through something, they have transcended it. Transcendence is about more than just opening your eyes and drawing breath every day. Transcendence is about processing negative thoughts and emotions for the purpose of understanding and forgiveness. I can say that it has taken many, many years for me to even come close to transcending the events surrounding losing my mother, but every day I move closer.

It's not about you. wait! maybe...it is?

For many in the metaphysics community (Metaphysics is the study or examination of the true nature of reality), [19] there is a notion of "raising universal consciousness," of increasing the critical mass of awareness of all human beings in hopes of improving the health of the world as a whole. At the core of this theory is the realization that both everything and nothing is about the individual, meaning that everything you do impacts another person...so truly your actions are not about you.

---

[19] Heartcompass Enterprises and The Foundation for A Mind and Heart. "Modern Metaphysics: Exploring the True Nature of Reality with Science and Technology. Accessed on January 5, 2013. http://www.metaphysics-for-life.com/modern-metaphysics.html.

However, because you are the actor, everything is about the way you handle a situation when you are in it. So you have to be healthy. You have to develop a healthy mind, with healthy habits or else everything around you will show signs of disease and chaos.

As we journey through this life, there will always be moments when we doubt ourselves, when we aren't sure how we ended up where we are doing what we are doing with whomever we are doing it. It happens. We can safely acknowledge our feelings of confusion and our impulses to destroy with our words, actions, thoughts, or intentions, but we don't have to act on them. Instead, we can take just a second to remember how we impact the world.

Here's a more practical example. It's about food. Remember how you felt when you went to order your double cheeseburger...the one you'd been thinking about all day? (On the off chance that you don't eat double cheeseburgers, think of some other delectable treat). So you pull up to the McDonalds, all the while savoring the delicious, mouth-watering cheeseburger, in your mind.

You order the double cheeseburger and the sales associate gives it to you—cold and hard. Nothing like the juicy little piece of heaven you anticipated. Just a dry, cold insult to what you had hoped for. Do you take it personally? Chances are the sales associate wasn't thinking about you...she was thinking about herself and how she hated her job.

You had nothing to do with the reason why she gave you a cold cheeseburger, but both your experience and appetite were ruined nonetheless. This is the simple reality that both everything and nothing is about you.

Believe me, I would love to find a loophole in universal law that makes it okay for me to do and say whatever I want and reap no consequences. I would love to believe that my acts of indiscretion have nothing to do with anyone but me…but deep down, I know each of us has the capacity to leave a lasting impact on other people—good, bad or ugly.

And while an addiction and a cold cheeseburger may seem a world apart, at the core they are both rooted in the same unconscious mind. A mind that is selfish and controlling. A mind that retaliates when confronted with unpleasant thoughts or realities. A mind that destroys itself. A mind that is not in touch with the spirit.

dedication

Once I had a firm grasp of the "dealing with pain" thing, coupled with the "everything and nothing is about me" thing, I was finally ready to address my addiction from a healing (and not just stopping) standpoint. I knew I would need to confront the issue that had triggered the addiction in the first place if I was ever going to stop huffing for good. I started the process by reintroducing my mom into my life the only way I knew how. I placed photos of her in public view and even put a picture of her on my altar.[20] Then, I worked up the courage to forgive myself for being ten years old at the time of her death. I forgave myself for not fully understanding what was happening to my mother in her last days. Most importantly, I chose to stop defining myself by my pain. I didn't want to be "Kenya, whose mom died" or "Kenya, who became an addict."

I wanted to be something else. Being a victim and an addict was a part of my past. I wanted to create a life for myself more in keeping with where I was going instead of where I had been.

I realize, however, that some people, especially those of us who have suffered a great loss, feel the process of healing is somehow like forgetting that our loved one existed. We want to keep the memory of our loved one alive, so we resolve to do it by rehashing our pain instead of celebrating our memories.

In order for me to transcend the loss of my mother, I had to understand that moving on did not mean forgetting. It simply meant that, as my mother's last gift to the world, I needed to be healthy.

My mother's addiction to cigarettes had killed her. Didn't I owe it to her to break that cycle and be healthy? Being healthy was the most fitting way to honor her memory.

---

[20] An altar is a sacred space. People oftentimes designate it as a place to pray. Some people also place pictures and/or items of ancestors or holy beings on their altar.

Not by punishing myself.

Until her dying breath, my mom would have given her life for me, and I wasn't about to let that sacrifice go to waste. I found a reason to quit, and the burning desire subsided. I didn't need it anymore. There was no reward in being a martyr. I began to understand that my healing started with me, just as the choice to be destructive did.

If I needed to take a moment to nurture, love, and appreciate myself, it was okay. I didn't need to punish myself forever. I could mourn my mother without carrying the weight of her death on my back for the rest of my life. I could forgive myself and still honor her.

As I write this, I have been clean for almost two years and I couldn't be more excited. I got clean by way of a process. For ten days, I fasted from all solid food and any habits that I deemed destructive (huffing, picking, gossiping, etc.). Not eating for ten days can be daunting, so I used some skills that I learned in my Narcotics Anonymous meetings to help me. In our NA meetings, we promise that "just for today" we will not use. "Just for today" we will make the healthy choice. During my fast, I dedicated each day to a virtue that I wanted to strengthen in myself. I did this to remind myself why I was doing what I was doing, and to stay focused on the life I wanted to create for myself.

There is a similar technique in Kadampa Buddhism called meditation dedication. Meditation dedication is when you conduct your prayers and intentions in honor of someone else.

Mondrub, my Buddhist meditation leader, told us to do this because for many people it's easier to unconditionally love and accept others than it is to unconditionally love ourselves.

Since becoming clean, I have expanded the practice of dedicating my days to virtues, to dedicating my days to loved ones. This allows me to remember that I am not the only person affected by my actions.

If you are seeking to rid yourself of a destructive habit, I suggest you adopt some variation of what I did. A great way to start is by fasting for a set amount of days, then dedicating the days during the fast. You can use a virtue, a person, or maybe even a long-time goal. You could also use the Tools of the Spirit that I have outlined in this book. I have found that it is easier to give up something bad when you have something good to focus on. Plus, it's much easier to see how superfluous your bad habit is when you are sacrificing something as significant as eating.

Lastly, here's an exercise you can do the next time you feel the urge to destroy yourself. Close your eyes and imagine someone whom you want the best for. Someone for whom you have nothing but pure love. You can use a lover or a child, maybe even a friend. Imagine you and your loved one together, enjoying each other, laughing and having fun. Imagine that person smiling. How does that make you feel? Good, right? I bet it makes you smile too. Now, take this same image of your smiling loved one, and imagine yourself doing to them what you are about to do to yourself.

Now, that feeling, the one you are feeling right now—that sick, eerie feeling that is coming over you as you think of hurting your loved one. That is the feeling of connection you were longing for in the first place. That is how you know you are not alone in this world. You love them, you could never do *that* to them.

Know that, where there is love, there is an opportunity to heal. You have just discovered your reason to turn away from all destructive behavior is this very moment. Truly, the end to your frustrations lies in your ability to allow good to come to you. Let go of all your negative beliefs and expectations. Stop defining yourself by the tragedies that have befallen you, and focus on the promise of transcendence. Dedicate your life, first to your healing, and then to the people and things you love most. Think of them before you hurt them or yourself with destructive words or actions.

And most importantly, remember you are alive. You are divine. As a living being, you are the antithesis of destruction. You are the miracle of creation!

Note to self
(and everybody else):
On Destruction

Life's situations and circumstances do not give me the license to be destructive. Instead, I become conscious of my surroundings, allowing peace, joy, and love to come to me.

In the face of opposition, I am the inspired **S P A C E** of Creation.

Conclusion

Now What?

"**Cognitive dissonance** is the state of holding two or more conflicting cognitions (e.g., ideas, beliefs, values or emotional reactions), simultaneously.[21]" During the quarterlife, we associate love with success, and failure with pain. We all want unconditional love and acceptance. Yet our attachments, judgments, and destructive tendencies cause us to fear never getting it. Accordingly, the quarterlife crisis is marked by severe **cognitive dissonance** surrounding our desire to experience unconditional love and to avoid pain. The dissonance is the product of our ego and spirit fighting to merge our passions with our perceptions.

We believe that our affiliations, also known as attachments and judgments, will somehow shield us from the pain we have come to expect. We think they will draw us closer to unconditional love and acceptance. However, at some point we realize that they can't and they won't. In this moment the anxiety begins. Because of this, our fears about the quarterlife crisis are often misunderstood. We are not afraid because we have not achieved a certain status or because we have not earned a certain amount of money. We are afraid

---

[21] L. Festinger, *A Theory of Cognitive Dissonance.* (Palo Alto, Calif.: Stanford University Press, 1957).

because deep down we know there is more to happiness than what we can possess.

In our hearts, we know that we will never experience unconditional love and acceptance if we continue to place countless conditions on our own worthiness. We also know that we cannot be the pure potentiality of the empty. S P A C E if we are constantly seeking a false sense of security from anything external.

In this state of dissonance, we experience many of the feelings that have come to define the quarterlife crisis— dread, guilt, anger, and embarrassment.

embrace the empty. S P A C E.

Prior to the quarterlife crisis, we chose to focus on potential instead of problems. In that S P A C E, there was no room for failure. So now that this picture has changed slightly, we must not let what appears to be real in the moment, become our life experience.

We are not a collection of longstanding ideas about what success *should* look and feel like. We are the empty. S P A C E that gives birth to both success and our ideas about failure. The beauty in being that S P A C E is that we can choose our focus. The experiences that we have been taught to judge as negative are just a part of our overall life experience. They will pass away and we will be just as whole as we were before they came to us. So, you cannot and *will not* be destroyed by this experience. Conversely, this experience will strengthen you. It will teach you to focus, with laser-light precision, on what you want (unconditional love and acceptance) even in the presence of what you don't (fear of failure).

All that exists in nature does so in a state of non-attachment and non-judgment. Think about it, when a tree dies there is no cosmic consequence and no ceremonial resistance from other trees. The trees do not resist because they know that death is a part of life. In the same way, we must understand that change is a part of the human experience. There is nothing and no one who has the power to define or destroy us. Created in the image of the great "I am"…we are. And just as our affiliations do not have the power to make us more of ourselves, they also do not have the power to make us less of ourselves.

No situation, circumstance, historic event, or Tool of the Ego has the power to threaten the true nature of who we are. They cannot hurt us. What they can do, on the other hand, is distort our focus. When we are experiencing the Tools of the Ego, our focus has been shifted from all that is big and beautiful about the whole of our experience to the tiny details of a part of it.

That's why the Tools of the Spirit are so helpful. The Tools of the Spirit are oriented to the larger part of who we are, the part of us that is without judgment or fear. The Tools of the Spirit remind us who we really are and what we really want.

Truthfully, it's all a matter of perspective anyway. Five years ago, during my quarterlife crisis, I thought my life was coming to an end. Now, as I look back, I am grateful for it. I know that, without this experience, I would have never stopped defining myself by what I had and who I thought I was. I would have never discovered empty. S P A C E, and I would have never written this book.

At our core, we are seeking alignment with source energy. Source energy offers no resistance to any part of itself. It knows that its parts do not have the power or intention to destroy its whole. It fears nothing. Source energy allows all that is—to be, without interference. Source energy does not fear the empty. S P A C E.

Take a moment to channel the fearlessness of source energy. In this moment, make a decision to appreciate the beauty around you. Learn to have compassion for your fellow human (and for yourself). Become enthusiastic about your life and create something beautiful! Just try it, and in time you will see:
This is not a crisis…it's an opportunity.

Take it.

Part 3:

reflections on crisis-this is my real life!

Two years ago, I started a blog. The blog was meant to be a safe place for me. It was a S P A C E where I could be myself without judgment. A place where I could be completely honest and exposed, and write whatever I felt, no matter what.

In the spirit of vulnerability, I offer you the following reflections. Each entry pays homage to the raw emotion, hopeless disparity and eventual transcendence that characterized my quarterlife crisis. These blogs are the essence of who I was, and they are the empty. S P A C E of who I came to be.

reflections on following your dreams

"Bitter – Party of One"
June 22, 2011 @ 8:47 AM

"What happens to a dream deferred?"

Does it dry up
like a raisin in the sun?
Or fester like a sore –
And then run?

…

Or does it explode?

– Langston Hughes

Or does it turn you into a mean bitter bitch?

As children, we all had a vision of what our lives would be
like. We knew what we wanted to do with absolute certainty.
Although the specifics of our vision may have changed over
time, from Power Ranger to pediatrician, the emotional
foundation of our vision doesn't usually change that much.
Truthfully, Power Rangers and pediatricians do the same
thing—save, help, and heal.

Unfortunately, as we age, we learn that six-year-old dreams
don't live long in twenty-six-year-old worlds. Sure, we try our
hardest to hold onto them, but in the midst of navigating the
intellectual and spiritual maze of life, "shit happens."

Bills happen. Family crises happen. Relationships happen. In short, life happens. Sometimes, life throws us a curve ball that causes us to deter or defer our dreams. We say that we will get back to saving the world once we pay off some debt, or get another degree. We plan to return to our dreams once our children reach a certain age, or when we find the right partner. These are all just distractions, excuses for us to wait and procrastinate.

In the meantime, we resolve to just get by. We get a job or find some other way to get our basic needs met, and the time just passes on. Until one day, we look up and we have become muted, complacent, and filled with anger and regret.

Last week, a close friend and I had a long overdue talk about negativity. I know her to be a beautiful, generous, and intelligent person. Lately though, her demeanor has been filled with a dark negativity. So much so, that it's clouding the person I know her to be. At the end of our talk, we realized that her attitude had more to do with frustration than it did with real anger. She, like me, is a creative spirit. She has had a hard time, however, finding the appropriate S P A C E to express her creativity. As the days pass and she is unable to harness and share those intimate parts of herself, the frustration builds. Eventually it erupts.

It's interesting how many of us can relate to this scenario. We were born to create. Just think about it, absolutely everything in existence came from the cultivation of an idea. Notice, I said cultivation of an idea. An idea all by itself can't do much. It's the cultivation that gives it power. A few years ago, I saw a picture of Bill Gates taken in 1978. The picture was of his original Microsoft employees. Thirty years later, I'm typing this blog on a Microsoft product and Bill Gates is one of the wealthiest men in the world. Of course, the story of how that happened is much more complicated than the space between those two sentences allows, but the simple reality of it is the same. Success requires both creativity and concentrated attention.

Builders must build and creators (human beings) must create. If we don't, it's easy to develop an angry disposition and a bad attitude. We are angry because we feel like we're wasting our lives, and not living up to our full potential. We have a nagging feeling that there is so much more to life than what we are experiencing. At the same time, we feel confused about how to get more out of our lives. Enter aggravation. Make sense?

I know that it's unrealistic to assume that we can all abandon the demands of our everyday lives to pursue what many of us have (now) been convinced is a pipe dream. I still think it's absolutely necessary for you to find an outlet for the creator in you. Ultimately, I would love to see everyone do only what makes them happy, to work only in careers that validate and celebrate them. That is definitely the goal. That may take some time though, so while we manifest that reality, here are a few things we can do to prevent ourselves from suffering from what I call "Creative Constipation."

1. *Express yourself* – Everyday there are a million billion thoughts running through our minds.

Only a few hundred thousand of those thoughts actually escape—either in speech or in action. So what happens to the rest? Some of them just pass away, but others keep coming back. Have you noticed that sometimes you have the same thoughts over and over? That is happening for a reason. Pay attention to what you think and to how you feel about your thoughts. Spend some time writing about your thoughts. If you're not a writer, talk about your thoughts—to yourself if you need to. If you're not a verbal or linguistic person you can express yourself in other ways. Try screaming, painting, drawing, singing. Make YouTube videos...whatever. Just find a way to get some of that million billion out.

2. *Separate love from money* – This is a tough one. Money is a big deal for almost everybody I know. Money is the reason we stay in the job that we don't love long after we've realized we don't love it. We need the money. I get it. However, when you're trying to remember what made you smile when you were six, money can't be the determining factor. As creators, we must first seek to create and trust that money will follow. Money can't really stop you from following your dreams, anyway.

Four years ago, I realized I wanted to be a writer. At the time, I was an executive for a large nonprofit (I hated it just as much as it hated me). I didn't pursue becoming a writer because I couldn't understand how I could make money from it. It took me three years to realize that being a writer is about writing, not money. A writer is, by definition someone who writes. Unpaid writers are still writers—are they not? So the next time you are thinking that you can't do what you want to do because of money, remember that money is a perk. You can do whatever you want to do. No one and nothing is stopping you. Do what you love. Do it well. Do it for free. The money will come.

3. *Volunteer* – How many times have you heard that, "the thing that you would do for free is your true passion?" What we weren't told is the next step. The next step is, to do it for free. Sounds simple I know. We have to come to a place where we are able to see that our possibilities are not limited by our pockets. If you have always wanted to work with children, you can. You may not be able to get paid for it in the beginning, but at least your emotional needs will be met. Once your emotional needs have been met, it will be easier for you to determine your next steps.

4. *Fantasize* – Just because we are adults, doesn't mean we have to let our imaginations die. Remember all form came from an idea (from

empty. S P A C E). Everything came from
nothing. Anything that we can see, touch, and
feel came from the mind of someone. Your
mind is capable of yielding great ideas as well,
if you let it roam around a little. I think that all
the suggestions above lend themselves to
fantasy, but if you are still having a hard time,
concentrated fantasy may work.

Sit down in a quiet place and write down what
your perfect life would look like. Do it for all
aspects of your life. Do one for your
relationship. Do one for your career. Do one for
your family. It may seem silly, but I assure you,
where you can go in your mind, you can go in
real life.

It's important that we take ourselves out of our
everyday monotony if we ever want to change
or improve our situation. Just exploring where
your mind takes you in fantasy can be a
powerful eye opener to the parts of your mind
that have been silenced by responsibility for so
long. Listen to yourself and pay attention to
what you say.

5. *Do better!* – In this moment, make a
commitment to bring your whole self and all of
your attention to what you are currently doing
for money. Begrudging your job won't make it
go away. It will only make your experience

worse. So agree to be grateful for what you
have. Do the best you can at what you do.
Show the Universe that you are grateful for
what you have and more will come.

Dreams and aspirations are a real part of our human
experience. Dreams are the mind's way of revealing to you all
that you are capable of doing. There is a powerful creator in
each of us waiting to be expressed and released. When we
neglect the creative parts of ourselves we become constipated,
confused, and oftentimes mad as hell. Mad at our jobs
because we have to go to them. Mad at the people who we
think have what we want. Mad at our parents and friends for
not understanding. Mad at ourselves for all of it. Just mad as
hell...all the time!

You may think that you don't have the time, energy, or
money to pursue what makes you happy, but I think you're
worth the sacrifice. How many hours, months, and years have
you spent doing what you should do and what was expected
of you? Now it's time for you to do what you want to do.

I hope these suggestions bring a little peace and purpose to
your life. Langston Hughes hit the nail on the head when he
suggested that a dream deferred explodes.
Don't let your unrealized dreams turn you into a walking time
bomb.

reflections on rejection

"Acceptance"
August 2, 2012 @ 1:27 PM

Yesterday was a very disturbing day for me. It was disturbing not only because I felt like my relationship was being attacked, but because of all the feelings of inadequacy that this particular argument stirs up within me. I felt judged and attacked. And because I felt judged and attacked...I wanted to judge and attack. I wanted to say mean things to the people who were saying mean things about me. I wanted to point out inconsistencies in their stories and convince them that their backwards way of thinking was both hurtful and wrong. I wanted to, but I didn't because I was afraid that if I was honest, both my kindness and my contempt would be taken the wrong way.

Today is a little different. I have had time to reflect, and in my reflection I have realized that much of my anger is really pain. Plus, I know that there is nothing I will ever be able to say to convince some people that loving another woman is right. But, I also know that "right" is relative. "Right" varies drastically depending on who you are talking to and what you are talking about. And since, "right" and "wrong" have no real place within a Universe that only recognizes "is"...my desire to be accepted doesn't really have much to do with being right either. It has to do with being honest and still feeling okay.

A lot of people say that they don't care what others think about them. That the only opinion that matters is their own (sometimes I wish I felt that way too). But part of me knows that much of my strength is my compassion. My being able to identify, understand, and empathize with other people is one of my favorite things about me. I don't want to lose that just because sometimes it hurts to be that way. Being honest with myself requires me to admit that what people think about me does matter. I want to feel valuable for who I am, and for what I bring to the people and spaces around me. I want my life, and my words to have a positive impact on the people I come into contact with.

Deep down, I believe that if people don't like me, I won't be successful. But if I don't like me, I may risk living in a perpetual state of fear and doubt. That being said, I have a choice to make. My choice is not to live in a perpetual state of fear and doubt. My choice is to be honest about both who I date *and* the fact that I *care* what other people think about it.

Will their feelings change my actions? Probably not.

Does that make it hurt any less? Absolutely not.

I am going to resist the urge to wrap this up and make it deep or pretty. I am going to fight the feeling to tie this to an affirmation or some sort of life lesson or takeaway. The truth is, I am in love with a woman that I want to marry. It hurts my feelings when people think I don't deserve that right. It hurts my feelings because there is a part of me that just wants to be accepted. I have no desire to change other people's opinions, religious affiliations, or values.

I want to be accepted because I am human first.

I want to be accepted because not being accepted can be lonely and painful.

I want to be accepted for the same reasons that everyone else does.

"Learning to Love my Kaye"
April 12, 2011 @ 6:43 PM

Sometimes the most abusive relationship is the one you have with yourself...

I grew up in Cleveland, Ohio. The weather was cold—the sky was dark. The people were hard and the women were strong. The economy was depressed and sunny days were few and far between. When I think about Cleveland, I remember walking back and forth to school with my mom on snowy days, my little boots making puddles in the dining room floor when we returned home. I remember being bundled up so tight that only my nose peeked out of my snowsuit. I also remember shoveling snow with my mom on winter mornings. I remember a lot about growing up in Cleveland, the cold darkness especially.

One of my most vivid memories, however, is of someone who has come to be one of my closest friends. Let's call her…ummm…Kaye. So in fourth grade, Kaye had a crush on a boy named "Brian." "Brian" was a very popular boy that could have had any little pigtailed fourth grader he wanted. However, nine year old Kaye wanted him to want her. So one day, after mustering up the courage, she asked him (via an intricately folded note of course) whether he liked her too. "Brian" was hesitant. He wrote back that he was still weighing his options on choosing a girlfriend, but he was willing to tell her who all the contenders were.

He said he would tap each girl (in order of cuteness) on the shoulder. Kaye watched with baited breath as he tapped "Michelle," "Imani," "Tiana," and then her (fourth and last). Kaye's heart dropped into her shoes, and her face cracked into a million pieces.

Kaye, with her chocolate skin and wooly hair, was a stark contrast to the bright skinned, spiral haired little girls that had been chosen before her. Was she really the fourth cutest girl in the fourth grade? The thought hurt. Bad. Kaye didn't really understand what was going on. The concept of being "pretty" had never occurred to her, much less the concept of ranking prettiness. She knew how to rank spelling ability and scores on social studies tests. She knew that her name was always listed at the top of the Honor Roll list. She also knew that she had eaten breakfast with the principal more times than any other student. But she had no clue, that cuteness could be measured, or how incredibly painful it was to *not* be number one in this category. This was the first time she felt the sting of rejection based on looks, but it wouldn't be the last.

The progression was as follows....

In elementary school, she was ranked fourth cutest.

In middle school, she was teased because her "press-and-curl" would never stay pressed or curled for longer than two days. All the other little girls' hair was bouncy and beautiful for at least a week.

In high school, she finally got the hair thing under control, (and by under control I mean she got a perm), but she was still darker than the other girls.

In college, she was told that she could only join the service sorority, because only pretty girls could join the other one. (Not that she even wanted to join the other one, but she didn't like the idea that she shouldn't because she didn't look the part).

In the midst of all these experiences, there was always some butterscotch beauty held up as the ideal. Kaye was just the smart accomplice, the girl in the background with the great sense of humor and the big butt. Boys never told her she was pretty, but instead commented on her curves, her personality, her intelligence, and her sex appeal. Kaye enjoyed the attention from men, but in the back of her mind, all she ever wanted was to feel beautiful. It took almost fifteen years for that to happen. But eventually, it did.

Upon moving to Atlanta (and realizing she was a lesbian), Kaye met a remarkable woman. This woman loved her deep brown skin, chestnut eyes, and thick puffy hair. Let's call her Ms. Remarkable. Ms. Remarkable never missed an opportunity to tell Kaye how beautiful she was inside and out. Her words would have made Kaye feel great, had she only believed them. But she didn't.

The attention made Kaye self-conscious and even angry at times. She thought this must be some sick joke. Of course, there was a prettier girl that Ms. Remarkable could and *should* date. Surely, Kaye was not good enough. Kaye's insecurity ultimately led her to seek solace outside of the relationship. She began to feel that if she could obtain a woman as pretty as she wished she was, maybe she would feel good enough to deserve Ms. Remarkable. So she sought to collect as many pretty women as friends (or more than friends) as she could. She prayed that their presence in her life would somehow fill the hole that had been festering in her soul for years.

On any given day, you could find her lurking around the local strip club or party, romancing and charming every creamy complexioned lady in the place. It made her feel good that they liked her. The only problem was that Ms. Remarkable felt like the whole flirting, spending time with, and on occasion sleeping with pretty ladies…was a bit like cheating. She didn't see this as a healthy form of therapy for

Kaye. Needless to say, before long, she left. When she did, Kaye was alone with her "trophies" and low self-esteem. Her relationship was over and Kaye was left with exactly what she thought she deserved. Nothing and no one.

Initially, Kaye wasn't even mad when Ms. Remarkable left her. In her heart of hearts, she didn't think she was good enough to be anyone's first choice, anyway. Being second, third or fourth was all she could expect. She shoved her feelings deep down and kept rummaging through strip clubs and bars collecting "beautiful things."

Three years passed, and all Kaye had to show for her new hobby was free admission to every club in the city and a drinking problem. Her self-esteem was still fractured and there had been no one since Ms. Remarkable that was willing to take on the responsibility of Kaye and her "dark-skinned-nappy-head" issues. Of course, Kaye was good enough to be the "best friend with benefits," or the chick you called after the club. She could be the chick you trusted with your deep dark secrets, but she was never the main chick. Never the wifey, or the one who got introduced to the family.

That was until the summer of 2009, when Kaye met a young lady more emotionally compromised than she was. The young lady, in truth, was beautiful. But after years of being abused and passed over because of her weight, she had no clue how beautiful she was. She was mean, angry, resentful, and incredibly volatile. She hid her insecurity under the guise of being a diva, constantly belittling and insulting everyone around her. As a result, their relationship was just as ugly as they both felt. They fought and cursed, both trying to hate each other as much as they both hated themselves. It was then that Kaye realized the root of her problems was her belief system.

Twenty years ago, Kaye had decided to believe that she wasn't pretty and therefore didn't deserve to be loved, respected, or chosen. As a result, the last twenty years of her life and her subsequent relationships had reinforced her beliefs. How could she expect anyone to see beauty in her if she was unable to see beauty in herself? Beyond that, who said she couldn't be all the things she had always been told she was, and still be beautiful. Couldn't she be smart and beautiful? Sweet and beautiful? Thoughtful and beautiful? Natural and beautiful? Dark-skinned and beautiful?

She asked herself, was she really willing to accept that there was only one type of beauty? Only the kind conceived in the mind of an eight year old boy?

What is more, was she comfortable believing, because she didn't possess a certain type of beauty, that she wasn't worthy of love and commitment? Didn't she deserve more?

She realized that the whole "you're not pretty, you're not worth it thing" was an agreement that she had made many years ago. As long as she agreed to keep this belief, her life would continue to reflect it. She sought out to change her belief, to see herself the way God saw her. Perfect.

I tell this story about my close friend Kaye because it's a constant reminder of the damage we do to ourselves with our thoughts and beliefs. Perhaps, you don't have "dark-skinned-nappy-head" issues like Kaye. Maybe you were the fat girl, the skinny girl, the below average student, the one with the lisp, or the kid who stuttered. Who knows what your struggle is, or if you even have one. The point is, all of us have a friend like Kaye. She's the part of us that tells us we can't. She's the voice of negativity that keeps us from running without fear toward our dreams. Kaye is the reason why we stay in bad relationships, unfulfilling work situations, and dead-end friendships. She is why we overeat, drink too much, or gossip about people. She is childhood negativity all grown up, living and breathing as you!

When you have a Kaye in your life (like most of us do), you can choose to do one of two things: you can choose to believe her or you can choose to love her. If you choose to believe her, you are agreeing that you are unworthy, non-deserving, and so on. On the other hand, if you choose to love Kaye, you are choosing to have compassion for her. Kaye did not pull her beliefs out of her behind. She developed these views because of what she was told and what she experienced. Kaye's attitude is the result of the pain. So, her healing can only be facilitated by love. Kaye needs to know that you love her anyway. She needs you to love all the parts of her that she has been told make her less than. If she believes you love her, maybe one day she will learn to love herself.

Admittedly, it has taken me years to love and accept my Kaye. And there are still moments when I can hear her teasing me about my complexion and my hair texture. In those moments, I tell her as gently and patiently as I know how, "I love you Kaye. I love all that you are and all you aren't. You are a part of me. You are more beautiful than words can articulate and more lovely than poets can describe. It's not your fault that kids are cruel or that the world can be one-sided and unfair."

It's true—I do love Kaye, because she is a part of me. She is the memory of my troubled and painful past. Kaye reminds me that sometimes beauty is fragile, just like nine year old hearts. If you don't handle them with care, spirits can be broken at the hands of one person's preference.

Now, Kaye and I are down like Brandy wanted to be, in 2002. Sometimes we argue. She thinks my hair is nappy, I tell her it's thick and strong. She thinks my skin is too dark, I tell her that the sun favors me, that's why I get so much "shine." She thinks I'm heavy; I remind her that Nicki Minaj paid to have a body like mine. At the end of the day we work together to create the being that is me.

Kenya... the girl who is not ashamed to confront her past, but not naïve enough to accept it as her current reality. Kaye taught me how to love myself, and for that I am forever in her debt.

All of our love,
Kenya (and Kaye)

how can you love the Kaye in you?

reflections on conforming

"Different...Just like everybody else"
January 21, 2012 @ 3:46 PM

"Come on…who do you….who do you think you are/ hahaha bless your soul/ you really think you're in control?"

– Gnarls Barkley, "Crazy"

From the time we were little kids, someone has been telling us what to do, where to go, and who to go there with. Our parents pick our schools. Our schools (indirectly) pick our friends. Our friends pick our habits. The television, magazines, and popular media pick our clothes and shoes. Our religion, race, and political affiliations fill in the blanks for everything else. So much of our lives are decided for us.

Have you ever noticed that? If not, take a moment now to consider it. I wanted to start this post off by posing this question, because it's the perfect segue to the larger issue of normalcy.

What do you think was the underlying motivation for all the decisions that were made for you as a child? It was normalcy. Your parents wanted you to fit in with other children, so they sent you to a good school, with other good children because they wanted you to be a good kid. They assumed all that goodness would rub off on you. It's the same reason why they wouldn't let you wear your Power

Ranger costume to school after Halloween. They didn't want people to laugh at you. But, as a result of all this sameness training, you learned a very important lesson—being normal is the goal.

Now, on the off chance that you *do* decide to be different, you will need to find a group a people that are different in the same way. It's the essence of social groups like Goths or gangs. Both groups are trying to convey deviance to the world, but all the members of the group do it the same way. The Goths, with their black lipstick and trench coats, and the gangs with their guns and violence. So original, right?

The point of all this is, in your pursuit to become normal, you decided that there are certain experiences and people that you need to have in your life. You need to go to *this* school, and marry *this* person. You need to join *this* group and be friends with *these* people. You think that having these things will make you successful and normal, but more than anything you think they will make you happy. Until, one of two things happens. You either don't get the things you think you need to be happy, or you do (and you are still unhappy).

If you don't get the things you think you need to be happy, you will obviously be upset. If you do get them, but are still unhappy, you will be confused and angry. "What! But why?" you will ask yourself. "Aren't I supposed to be happy? Wasn't the job supposed to make me happy? What about the husband/wife? Or the baby? You will wonder, "Didn't this make all the other people happy? " "Is there something wrong with me because I have these things and am not happy?"

You may even be told by others that you are ungrateful because you are not happy. You may begin to feel guilty. Sound familiar? I know it does for me.

At the core of all this normalcy and unhappiness is comfort and fear. These were even the two underlying factors in your parents' motivation to make you normal in the first place. They were afraid that people would make fun of you for being different, so they taught you to conform.

As we get older, we get so comfortable in doing "the right thing" that we forget to do what we *think* and *feel* is right for us. In truth, there is nothing wrong with wanting a traditional lifestyle. But if you don't feel like that's a good fit for you, that's okay too. Human beings are just as different as we are alike. Ponder that. There is no person, living or dead, that is just like you and there never was. I truly believe that we are here on this earth to have an exchange with each other. A cultural, spiritual, and sometimes physical exchange; one where we both learn from and teach each other. The purpose is definitely not to morph into carbon copies of each other.

The other day, I read a post from one my favorite bloggers.[22] The post was about her decision to leave her job and pursue a career in creativity. In the post, she spoke about

---

[22] The name of the blog is "Dream. Delight. Inspire," and the blogger's name is Kimberley.

how loosing the comfort and normalcy of her job was causing her to panic. She said she was worried about money and bills. I could relate to her post and thought it served as a great lesson for all of us.

How many of us have devoted our whole lives to a career, lifestyle, religion, or idea that just isn't working for us? Yet, we refuse to change. We refuse to try something different for fear of rejection or failure. Is our fear of unpredictability and not fitting in stronger than our will to be happy? Stronger than our desire to create?

The Bible says that you can't serve two masters, and I believe this to be true. You can't have a desire to fit in at all costs, and then expect for wonderful marvelous things to manifest in your life. It just doesn't work that way. Being marvelous takes a leap of faith. It takes courage and a desire to be the one who makes the trends instead of the one who mindlessly follows them.

Now, don't get me wrong, I am definitely talking to myself as well. I sometimes sneak and apply for jobs every now and again, trying to convince myself that something will feel better than my fingers tapping on this keyboard. Or that something else will warm my soul like finishing a poem, blog posting, or a chapter in my book. But the truth is, nothing feels better. I don't castigate myself for that anymore either. I just accept me for me.

I challenge you today to believe in yourself enough to explore the possibility of doing something you have always wanted to do, but didn't because you were scared. Do it. Do it today. Why not?

You have been doing things the same way for this long and what has it gotten you? More of the same, right? So you can cut the hair you have been growing since you were twelve. Go back to school for marine biology if you want. You're not a "crazy" weirdo just because you're interested in yoga, or want to take up swing-dancing. Even if you want to leave your job and bake cakes for a living. It's okay. There are no cruel kids waiting to tease you or beat you up, I promise!

what's "abnormal" about you?

reflections on letting go

"Pressure and Release"
August 25, 2011 @ 10:58 AM

I had a breakdown this morning. A crying till I couldn't
breathe, yelling and cursing type of breakdown. Please don't
be alarmed. This happens every few months. I guess it's my
way of releasing all that I hold in on a daily basis. Plus, I
knew it was coming. I've felt kind of crappy for the past few
days and have had a hard time sleeping. I'm guessing some
of it is withdrawal from all crap I've eliminated from my
diet. Today, however, my figurative "poopiness" was
overshadowed by a more literal one.

Today, courtesy of GROUPON Atlanta, I got my first
colonic. Yes, I said colonic. You know, the whole colon
hydrotherapy thing where they hook you up to a machine
and "help" you release waste? Yep, that's the one. Initially, I
wanted to do it because of this muffin top I can see rising
beneath my belly button. But in light of my current
emotional state, I thought maybe it could help me in other
ways too. I once read that excess waste in the body can
contribute to a bad attitude. I desperately wanted to lose
both, so I threw my inhibitions to the side and bought the
clean colon coupon.

Want to hear about it? Sure you do. Let's begin.
I arrived at the Wellness Center at 1:10 PM sharp. (I say
sharp because it makes me feel better about being ten

minutes late—lol… isn't that a cool trick)? The outside was a little sketchy, but the inside more than made up. Everyone was so happy and pleasant. I wondered if I would be happy too, once I wasn't "full of it" anymore.

I was still scared though. And when I'm scared I overcompensate. So, instead of just throwing on sweats and a t-shirt, I went all out for the occasion. I mean, I wore a sexy shirt with lots of cleavage and heels. Oh, and a ton of perfume. I don't know why I did that. I guess I figured if these people work in a colon clinic all day, I should ease their mind a little by assuring them that I was clean. My nerves, however, were nowhere near as composed. I tried to make awkward conversation, but the whole time I kept envisioning a tube the size of a water bottle impaling me—then drowning me from the inside. It was so weird and scary.

The experience made me think that even though others seem to be completely enthralled by my backside, I pretty much stay away from it. I think I may even resent my butt a little. It's a little too arrogant for me. It always wants to be seen and get all the attention. It's such a selfish little bugger that makes my pants tight. Blah. To be honest, the only time me and my rear-end really interact is when I am trying to coerce it into my Spanx. As such, you can only imagine my terror when I found out that the colonic machine was client operated. I thought, "You want me to put what, where? Why can't you do it?"

Quite honestly, I thought about asking them to do it for me. I quickly abandoned that idea though, because I didn't want to seem like some sick pervert who wears too much perfume and asks for personal favors from the staff. *takes deep breath* I knew I had to do it myself. So I took off my big girl pants and decided to deal with it.

I am pleased to say that my experience was nothing like I expected. The tube was smaller than my pinky finger, more like a straw. They also put special ointment on it to make the process smooth and easy. Once I laid down, soothing music was played and they placed a Kleenex with drops of lavender under my nose. The scent was so relaxing. The cool thing was I was in control of the water pressure the whole time. When I felt "full," I could either push or decrease the water flow altogether. I decided to do a little exercise in my head while I was on the machine. I imagined myself releasing all the things that had been clogging me up emotionally. I pictured the drama and stressors of my life being washed away into oblivion. It worked, and before I knew it my hour was up and I was getting dressed, (only this time I was one and a half pounds lighter).

When I was walking out, I said a silent prayer that my physical elimination would soon give way to a spiritual one.

I think my experience today is a bit of a metaphor. I'm sure all of us have things and people in our lives that make us feel…constipated. Sometimes these people and things are so close to us they can feel like a part of us. A part of us that we can't eliminate without significant work and some discomfort. Sometimes our fear of detachment is so great that we continue to cling to it, even though it makes us sick. I get it. Still, it surprises me how much metaphorical waste we can carry, and never even notice it. That is until it manifests on the outside—in the form of a crying spell or a chubby tummy.

After today, I can't help but think. What if we didn't ignore the signs? What if we didn't cower from the discomfort? What if the next time we felt a pressure so great we could see it in our body...we simply turned on some music, lit a candle, got in a comfortable position and let it all go…

how do you get rid of the crap in your life?

"Easier Said than Done"
October 10, 2011 @ 4:46 PM

What a difference a week makes...

Last week, I was on cloud nine. I was excited about submitting my proposal[23] and closing a chapter of my life

---

[23] In the fall of 2011, I participated in the Hay House Writer's Workshop, a book publication competition.

that has consumed me for sixth months. This week, I am
having a much harder time. I started a new job a few weeks
ago and to be quite honest the money is nothing like I
thought it would be. Beyond that, with no proposal to work
on, I am not doing much of anything with my time. When I
am not at work, I have been spending a lot of time "extreme
couch sitting," and "marathon TV watching." Blah. I guess
the job thing is really wearing on me because I feel like I
have been here before, and I am just not in the mood to deal
with it again.

People around me keep telling me to be patient because it's a
new spot and it could potentially pick up in the coming
months. My only issue with that is, the whole "could pick up
thing" doesn't really work well with my "definitely due"
bills. Georgia Power isn't interested in what *may* happen.
They want their money and so do I. On the other hand, I do
have quite a bit of money saved, so the money isn't as big of
an issue as the uncertainty and inconsistency. I am just so
over it. People keep telling me this is all temporary, but part
of me feels like that's the problem.

Since I have been in Atlanta, I have had one temporary job
after another. Not to mention, I have been let go from the
majority of those jobs. Double blah.

So anyway, I am struggling with all this because I want
more than anything to be done with the struggle of
constantly looking for something else. I just kind of want to
get somewhere and stay, you know? Of course, ultimately I
want to be a life coach and a writer but there isn't really a

track for that per se. So here I am again, out here in the wind, trying to make it work and keep my sanity in the process. It is hard.

Since I have had so many jobs in the past, the prospect of looking for a new one just seems sickening. I don't want to go back to corporate America because I am not a fan of being someone's "do-girl" puppet. I don't want to constantly have to prove I deserve my job by giving all of myself to some scheme pretending to be a cause. I'm also not really trying to get another serving job. I have had enough of the late nights and sore feet. I don't know, I guess this is what happens when you are on the verge of something big. Part of me feels like I won't be satisfied until I get what I want. I am just tired of being a hamster in a cage, running in a f***ing circle. I just want to be where I want to be...doing what I want to do. Now.

This past week, I felt so overwhelmed, I couldn't even cry. What's worse is that in the midst of me feeling like crap on the inside, I've beating myself up about it. I know that feeling like crap only attracts more crap. So what's a girl to do? I wish I had the answer, but I don't. And that's why I wanted to write to you guys. I want you to know that everyone has these same issues. At first, I was a little hesitant because I know how much we all like to think some people have it all figured it out, and when they don't, it can be disappointing. (I really want to have it all figured it, by the way, for you and for me). But, I never want to be the type of person that acts like they are above life and the situations that confront them. I'm not. This quarterlife crisis thing is no pushover. She is a sturdy 'lil you-know-what!

What comforts me most in moments like these is the fact that I still have the clarity to be honest and understand what is going on in my head. For me, understanding is half the battle. I am getting better at it...and as I get better..."it" gets better. In the meantime, I've learned that some things are easier said than done. I have learned that sometimes it's okay to stop moving and starting talking. Words are powerful, more powerful than I think many of us realize.

They say that all things in the Universe happen with speed and ease. So if something feels, "easier said than done," maybe it is. Maybe, declaring what you want can be the first step toward seeing it manifest in your life? Consequently, on days like today I resolve not to run around the city looking for a new "last" job. Instead, I go to my altar, light a yellow candle for enthusiasm, and I talk to God. I tell the Universe and my higher self what I want. I tell it how I want to feel, and what I expect. What is more, I pray in thanksgiving. Meaning, I speak as if what I am asking for has already manifested. I prefer it this way because it keeps my prayers hopeful instead of hopeless. I guess you don't always need to know *what* to do. Sometimes it's okay just to remember what to say and who to say it to.

Every morning, I pray in the shower. Below, I have included the prayer I said today.

Universe, S P A C E, and Silence: I pray in thanksgiving for another day just to live and exist in your kingdom. I pray in thanksgiving for a spirit of abundance in all areas of my life. I pray that anything and anyone that is not of you be removed from my physical and emotional S P A C E. I pray for an end to struggle. I pray in thanksgiving for clarity, understanding, and peace surrounding my current situation. I pray in thanksgiving for being a living representation of you and your love, to anyone I come in contact with. I pray in thanksgiving for my book contract and my book advance. I pray in thanksgiving for the health and strength of all my relationships. I pray that you bring my partner and I closer to you, each other, and our higher selves. Please guide my every word, thought, and action in your way. And if there is anything I forgot to pray for, please pray for it for me. I love you dear God, be with me at all times. Amen."

what do you say, when you don't know what to do?

reflections on personal responsibility

"When no one is looking"
November 11, 2011 @ 1:56 PM

About a month ago, I joined a running group called Black Girls RUN! Atlanta. BGR-A! is a chapter of the national fitness organization, Black Girls RUN! The Atlanta chapter has more than 3,500 [24] members—making it the largest running group in Georgia. Because of this, you can imagine how scared I was to join. I thought I would be the slowest, fattest, most out of shape girl in the whole group. Fortunately, my desire to be in the best shape of my life by my thirtieth birthday was greater than my fear of embarrassment. So I did it anyway, and of course I wasn't any of those negative adjectives listed above.

The experience has been wonderful. I could barely run a mile before I joined and now I can run three miles comfortably. Yeah, I am getting it in.

Last week was the Atlanta Marathon and Marathon Relay. The course is 26.2 miles. You could either run it alone or you could run it as a part of a relay team. Something like seventeen of the teams that were participating in the relay were from BGR-A! Those of us who were not running were asked to come out and cheer for the other members. It was so cool and a lot more emotional than I thought it would be.

---

[24] The number has since grown to 10,401 members.

I was proud to be there rooting for my BGR sisters and imaging myself participating next year. At the end, the entire group took pictures and chanted. It was so uplifting to see all those Black women coming together for something positive.

I was moved. I was so moved that I ran three miles after I left the group. After my run, I read something on the BGR-A! Facebook page, that moved me even more. One of the runners posted something along the lines of, "you have to run and practice all the time, not just when people are looking." I thought her words would provide the perfect topic for my blog today.

The person who posted the aforementioned quote recently finished a half marathon. Yesterday, she said that she completed her last mile in seven minutes and twenty seconds! Can you imagine the amount of training, discipline, and heart it takes to do that? I am sure she was excited to see us cheering for her at the end, but we were not on the course the entire time. She had to motivate herself. No one would have known if she had stopped or walked. Even now, I can't say for sure that she didn't (I doubt it though, since her team came in eighth out of 100). My point is she did what she had to do, because she had a promise to keep to herself.

I loved her post so much because it spoke to my own journey to lose weight and become a life coach. In life coach class, our teacher told us that the first portion of the class is called YOU-ology. My class is called Kenya-ology, and that is literally how I am supposed to refer to it. Why? Because I must first heal myself before I can help anybody else. There is no audience for that healing. When you are in the trenches of your physical and emotional transformation, there is no one there to cheer you on. It's just you, your memories, and your will to do better. That brings me to (drum roll please) this week's epiphany.

solo.

About two weeks ago, I started doing a little exercise on my blog called the #30daythankyou.[25] I started it on the anniversary of my mother's death. My mom passed when she was only forty-two years old, so as I approach thirty, I am more and more aware of how important it is to give people their flowers while they are still here to smell them. Beyond that, I love the way it makes me feel to tell someone thank you. I have found that it feels good to the giver and to the receiver. I was excited about my little activity and really expected that everybody in the world would get on board. However, quite the opposite happened. Only one of my ten closest friends has done it more than once (even after I asked). Part of me is really hurt, but in the moments I feel most alone, I try to remember two things. 1. God is all there is. 2. So what.

So what, if the people who I thought would support me don't. There are so many other people supporting me. So what, if this road feels lonely and hard sometimes. The true

---

[25] The #30daythankyou was an exercise that asked participants to publicly thank someone different (via social media) everyday for thirty days.

measure of my person is not in how many "fireworks"[26] I have. It's in the work that I do, when there is no cheering section. It's a tough space for me, but it's necessary.

There is a lot of shame associated with the quarterlife crisis. People don't want to talk about the uncomfortable feelings that come with being confused, unemployed, single, and broke. Some people won't even publicly join this community, because they don't want to be known as someone who can identify with these feelings. Some people may even be too busy, selfish, or absent-minded to participant in an exercise like this. I can understand that. Believe me, I get it.

What I also get is, at the end of the day the only people I have to be accountable to is myself and God. Since God is just a manifestation of my higher self, it all comes back to me again. There will always be people to clap for me at the end. People to wear t-shirts and take pictures and to say they, "knew me when." I am grateful to them for lending me their cheers...later on. I just can't afford to wait for those cheers to start.

I started studying metaphysics because I was a depressed, overweight, unemployed, single addict. I didn't think there would be a blog or a book. I just didn't want to feel sad anymore. Period. Now, more than five years later, I am clean, in love, and officially not overweight. In truth, there

---

[26] The term "fireworks" refers to the readers of my blog. It is a nod to the popular Katy Perry song, "Firework."

was no one there when I cried and threw up for hours as I withdrew from huffing, or when I lit candles on my altar for a year praying for a soul mate. No one was there when I stopped eating solid food for two weeks, trying to jump start my sobriety and my weight loss. I did it. It was hard, but I did it. I don't know why I thought writing a book would be any different? I know that I am a part of a whole, but I also know that I must do my best to keep *my part*—whole.

I now know that this life is my marathon, so I am just going to keep running. Even when I am alone. Even when I am tired, and long after everyone has gone home. I don't need a fan club to be a star or a cheering section to be a winner— and neither do you.

what do you do when no one is looking?

"The Biggest Loser"
January 14, 2011 @ 6:57 AM

A few months ago, one of my best friends was asked to be a trustee for our undergraduate university. Another one of my closest friends is thinking of going to Japan to teach.

One of my line sisters [27] is currently overseas discovering herself, starring in her own personal rendition of *Eat, Pray, Love*. All of my Facebook friends are married, engaged, or pregnant (even the gay ones). Meanwhile, I wait tables for money. Am I The Biggest Loser?

I thought it was important for me to share my thoughts with you on this matter because, in my opinion, much of the quarterlife crisis is about the perception of success. Be it in our relationships or our careers, we have all measured ourselves by the achievements of other people. We wonder, "when will it be my turn to shine?" Will I ever be featured in my Alma Mater's magazine? Am I inspiring others and living my best life?

This morning, I was all wrapped up in my thoughts, stuck somewhere between jumping off the curb and trying to slit my wrist with a nail file, when suddenly, I got an overwhelming feeling of joy. I realized, I do have something major to celebrate. I am healthy. More importantly, I am clean!

In earlier posts and in my book, I've discussed my history of addiction. I haven't gone into much detail because, I mean, we're all adults—we know what addiction means. My substance of choice isn't really relevant. What's important is

---

[27] "Line sister" is a term used within historically Black sororities .The term is used to refer to members who were a part of the same pledge class, or "line."

how I have allowed my addiction to control me for over half my life. I was secretive, and destructive. I was a liar and my emotions were always out of control. I was irresponsible, impulsive, and depressed. The people I kept company with only reinforced my destructive behavior, but I won't blame them. It's not their fault—they were products of my desire. Metaphorical nails to my magnet.

I know it's corny, but I actually tape *The Biggest Loser* every week. I watch all two hours in a trance like state. It's my favorite show! I love it for a lot of reasons, but primarily because its merit based. Meaning that, there are no ridiculous, underhanded alliances involved. Either you lose the weight or you don't.

Watching the show has inspired me greatly, not just to lose weight but to love myself and make life affirming choices. Now, when I make decisions about what to put in my body, I am more discerning. As a result, I gave some stuff up.

I gave up Coca-Cola *tear* and fried food for my complexion. I stopped drinking so much because I sincerely believe that a sober mind is a healthy mind. I even took an inadvertent hiatus from the club. No judgment though, because on my birthday, I plan to shake a tail feather on somebody's dance floor. I may even have a celebratory shot with my red wine. So, don't judge me.

My point is, I am changing my life. It's no secret that my desire is to be an author. I am motivated to help people by giving the unknown and unseen a voice and a spotlight. No one expects the Delta with a master's degree to be gay or struggle with addiction. The same way no one expects for young people to silently measure their personal worth by comparing their relationships, careers, homes, and cars to their peers. No one expects it, but we all know it happens. Against our better judgment, many of us strive to live a fairy tale. This fairytale is oftentimes rooted in tradition and normalcy. It doesn't work. We all have a different path, and we don't get to take mental or emotional field trips to other people's path.

In the past, I have been extremely successful in the eyes of the world. I have held national offices, won poetry competitions, directed districts, made really great money, worked for major companies, and garnered the respect and admiration of hundreds of people. However, in the midst of all that, I was broken and depressed spiritually. Now, as I am standing at the summit of my largest obstacle, I understand why things had to happen the way they did. I needed to lose some things, some habits, and some people in order to prepare myself for what I really wanted. Today, I am proud to say that I am happier, healthier, and more stable than I have ever been.

The Biggest Loser has taught me that sometimes you have to overcome yourself before venturing out to conquer the world. For some people, that process starts with something as simple, as knowing what *not* to put in their mouth. Still, who among us can say that losing hundreds of pounds isn't a feat?

In the end, all of our bad habits and unhealthy lifestyle choices are dead weight. I love the metaphor of loosing because when you lose something, you have no memory of where you left it. You know you had it, but you don't have the ability to use it anymore. When something is lost, it's useless. Take a moment and imagine a habit that you want to overcome. Pretend that you lost it and make up a sentence about it. Your sentence will go like this, "I am so happy that I lost my_____." Doesn't that feel good? Sometimes you have to "lose" in order to "gain."

Even if you haven't landed the perfect job or mate, remember you are still valuable, beautiful, priceless, relevant, and successful. Have faith that the path you're on is the right one. Use this time to hone, perfect, and nurture the work of art that is you. Make healthy choices, eat good food, create, express, and lose your desire for all that has ever held you back in the past. Commit to becoming a world class loser. This way when the awesomeness you have been manifesting comes knocking on your door, you will be ready inside and out. The process may not be easy and some people may seem to get there before you but...never underestimate the magnitude of your progress.

Robert Frost has a poem called "Stopping by the Woods on a Snowy Evening," It's one of my favorites. In it, he details an evening walking in the woods with his mule. He is admiring the beauty of the woods, when he remembers that he has other plans. He wants to stay longer but he knows that he can't. I wanted to include the last few lines of the poem, because they do a great job of capturing the subtle beauty of sacrifice for something greater.

> "The woods are lovely, dark and deep.
> But I have promises to keep,
> And miles to go before I sleep,
> And miles to go before I sleep. "

It's great to admire the achievements of other people. It's also good to congratulate them on all that they are achieving. Just make sure that you don't let their progress keep you from yours. Keep moving, and keep progressing. We all have promises to keep, both to ourselves and to the Universe.

what are you willing to lose?

reflections on addiction

"A sober mind is a healthy mind"
August 3, 2011 @ 10:12 AM

The past few weeks, I have been in a terrible rut. At first, I didn't want to admit it, but the moment I stepped on the scale and saw 175 in front of my little brown toes, I couldn't ignore it anymore. Something was wrong. The truth was, lately, if I wasn't at work, all I wanted to do was sleep or watch TV. But I couldn't put my finger on exactly what it was that was bothering me. Honestly, I can't say that much has changed in that respect. What I do know, however, is that I have been here before, in that limbo S P A C E on the verge of destruction. Not quite over the edge, but flirting with disaster. It usually starts with the food, and then comes the alcohol and constant partying. Who even wants to think about what comes after that.

I guess deep down, I know that some of my destructive behavior is due to my anxiety about submitting my book proposal to Hay House. I have never wanted something so bad, and the fact that it's starring me in my face is petrifying. As I said before though, I am not afraid of fear. I am not going to let myself screw this up.

Last year, while meditating in class, I had what some would call "inspired thought." In a voice clear as day, I heard something say "A sober mind is a healthy mind." The words haunted me.

At the time, I was still huffing and the concept of being sober was almost surreal. I wasn't sure that I could do it. So, I started off with an experiment. In the thirty days preceding my birthday, I stopped drinking and going out. I should mention that I did not want to do this. I put it off for months. The result was powerful. I felt a renewed focus and a renewed confidence in what I could do for me. Confidence is important when you are working toward a goal, so I know what I have to do.

Now at first glance being sober for thirty days may seem simple, but it's not for me. I work in a bar for Pete's sake. A bar full of rude, disrespectful, cheap you-know-what's. I usually have a drink everyday just to keep my temper under control. What I'm noticing though, is that pacifying myself is not allowing me to do the spiritual work I need to do. That has to stop. I need some discipline and some focus. So, I'm going to do another cleanse. No drinking and no going out for the next thirty days.

This whole healthy lifestyle thing is a process, complete with its own set of ups and downs. We have to be diligent and proactive. When we see something wrong, we have to address it, or risk it getting too big to manage. For me, the fear of blowing a chance of a lifetime or relapsing is unconscionable.

In preparation for my cleanse, I did a few things.

1. *Clean house/Wash clothes:* When you are trying to reset yourself it's important that you

do so in a space conducive for creation. You need a mental, physical, and spiritual clean slate. I also washed my hair, shaved my legs, and got my eyebrows done. Nothing feels better than a smooth clean body to match my new clean surroundings.

2. *Create a plan:* A month may not seem like a long time, but when you are planning to deviate from your regularly scheduled program, you have to have a plan. Otherwise, it's easy to fall back into bad habits. I have four picked virtues (one for each week) to govern my mind and activities while I am cleansing. I also have set little goals for myself to motivate me on the way. For example, I am planning to perfect a section of my book proposal each week in hopes of having it ready for editing by September first.

3. *Get a spiritual focus*: As a writer and a person of faith, words of affirmation are a major part of my life. In keeping with that, I wrote a little prayer for myself to recite twice daily. The words are meant to remind me why I am doing what I'm doing.

I am also planning to fit eating right and working out into my regimen, but I am not going to stress myself too much about that. This is about cleansing and redirecting, not punishing. This is my process. Welcome to it! I hope you enjoy. I'll be posting videos and some blogs about my feelings along the way. Wish me luck.

Oh, and I have included my Healthy Mind prayer below. It's like my own personal little mission statement. Maybe you can rearrange the words for your life. As for me, I'm off to drink some orange juice!

"A Healthy Mind"

A healthy mind is a sober mind.
A sober mind is a mind that does not take
alcohol in excess and is free of huffing.
A healthy mind is a mind that seeks to create,
and not destroy.
I have a sober mind.

A healthy mind yields healthy thoughts.
Healthy thoughts are free from addiction.
Healthy thoughts lift me up and make me feel
good about myself.
I have healthy thoughts.

A healthy mind has healthy conversations.
Healthy conversations do not revolve around
negativity.
I have healthy conversations.
A healthy mind yields healthy habits.
Healthy habits include getting a good's nights
rest and spending my time on constructive and
productive activities.
I have healthy habits.

A healthy mind needs a healthy diet

*A healthy diet includes leafy greens, fresh
vegetables, and lean proteins.
A healthy diet also includes ample water and
other natural beverages.
I have a healthy diet.*

*A healthy mind needs healthy relationships.
Healthy relationships enrich my life with
mutual laughter, love, appreciation, humor,
affection, inspiration, and responsibility.
Healthy romantic relationships include a
healthy sex life, where I am free to express
myself sexually without restraint or shame.
I have healthy relationships.*

*A healthy mind is a happy mind.
A happy mind expects good to manifest from
all situations.
A happy mind lives and experiences the world
through abundance,
an abundance of love, peace, finances,
inspiration and activity.
A happy mind is necessary for a happy self.*

*I have a sober mind,
with healthy thoughts,
healthy conversations,
healthy habits,
a healthy diet,
and healthy relationships.*

I am healthy and happy.

"Stronger"
January 24, 2012 @ 9:24 AM

"What doesn't kill you makes you stronger
stand a little taller.
Doesn't mean I'm lonely when I'm alone. "

– Kelly Clarkson

I have been an addict all my life. Over the years, I have tried to quit on several occasions, but I have never been successful for more than a few months. This time, however, I have been clean for over a year! While getting clean, I noticed something disturbing. As, I relinquished one addiction, I picked up another. I went from huffing to drinking—from drinking to womanizing—from womanizing to overeating. It was like I always needed something to attach to. My attachments kept me from being alone with my stress. Little by little, however, I have been peeling back the layers of my psyche. I have taken great care to learn why I do what I do.

In that process, I have learned that many of us will have one major and possibly singular struggle, for our whole lives. For some it's weight...for others it's self esteem, bad relationships, or money. I think that our plight in life is to stare whatever that thing is in the face and tell it, "I am not scared of you." Even so, severing yourself from your struggle can take time. For those who have battled with any of the issues above, you can understand that when you have

168

an unhealthy relationship with something, it can feel like a romantic relationship. You feel sad and lonely without it.

Think about it, food addicts love their food. They want to eat alone because they have an emotional connection with it. That being said, learning to have a healthy relationship with food can feel like a break-up and it can be very lonely. When I stopped huffing, I felt completely alone at first. I felt like no one understood me and I had no clue how to deal with my own emotions.

In hindsight, I know that my relationship with drugs, alcohol, women, and food was just my way of coping with my feelings. For years, it was my bad habits that defined me. I thought I would die without them, but not anymore. It is so hard to refrain from doing what you have always done, but at some point you have to break up with the pain of the past and go it alone. That being said, I wanted to post the lyrics to my new favorite song, "Stronger," by Kelly Clarkson. When I sing this song, I subconsciously dedicate it to the huffing, the food, the girls, the alcohol, and all the other stuff I thought I needed. I say thought, because today I realized, I was clean at a healthy weight in committed relationship and not dead.

What doesn't kill you makes you stronger!

what is making you stronger?

reflections on the quarterlife crisis

"Pissed the F*** Off"
February 9, 2012 @ 12:34 PM

I'm mad. Most days, I am *really* mad. I try not to complain, but feeling like I can't or shouldn't complain just makes me angrier. When I call people on the phone, they always want to talk about their problems or give me advice, which is also frustrating. So, I decided to vent here, about all the things that have been making me mad, stressing me out, and causing me to become a nervous wreck. I tried to channel and organize my thoughts, because some things lead to other things. Anyway, here is all the "stuff" that is on my mind right now. I tried to be as honest as possible. Seeing it all here makes me feel a little better. Feel free to comment and add what you're pissed about.

At my core, I am having a hard time recovering from this...

"a dream deferred" stuff

I wrote a great book and I can't get an agent because my platform isn't big enough.

I don't know how to make my platform bigger because it seems like young people are only interested in pop culture and celebrity gossip.

I feel like I can't identify, relate, or connect with them, because I am *not* interested in pop culture or celebrity gossip.

Plus, people who have written absolute trash get book deals and reality TV shows all the time. (Because people love trash).

So, I decided to use my degree and I got pissed off about….

career stuff

I have a Master's degree and a part time job.

For the first time in my life I love my job.

But it's part time…

and I need more money…

Which makes me have to deal with…

money stuff

I owe over more than $89,000 in student loans and have never made enough money to pay for them.

I have been in feast or famine mode for the past six years. Meaning I have a job for a year or two, get caught up on my bills, then lose my job and get behind again.

Five months ago, I had roughly $5,000 saved (then I lost my job), and now I have less than $500.

I owe more on my car than it's worth.

I'm scared I will never have enough.
I am scared to be angry about possibly never having enough, because I don't want to attract what I don't want. (It's hard not to think about what I don't want).

I don't want to have to waitress again. Or have to get two part time jobs. Or one temporary full time job while I look for another one.

None of the shit mentioned above is fair.

But you need money to live, which leads me to how pissed I am about…

job stuff (there is a difference between a job and a career)

I made more than $1,200 a week as a waitress, but had no insurance, no job security, and no pride in what I was doing.

So, I quit serving to do work that was more "legitimate" and now I make considerably less and it's taxed.

I know I haven't gotten certain serving jobs at certain places because of my skin tone and my hair texture.

I refuse to perm my hair and wear a weave to get into those places (but it still makes me feel bad).

My hair is so hard to deal with. It's thick and long and a pain in my ass!

And of course there is always….

body stuff

I run—a lot—and I am still not losing any weight.

People tell me I have a great body just because my butt is big.
All my clothes are too tight, and I look like a stripper, because not only is my butt big but so are my boobs and my legs.

But people think that's a good problem to have and they are always trivializing how being seen as a sex object makes me feel. (I'm scared that's all people see when they look at me)…

Come to think of it, people are always doing and saying stupid, inconsiderate stuff

like…

People are always telling me to smile. Shut the f*** up…you don't know my life.

173

People don't comment on my blog, although I know they read it.

People are always telling me that this situation is only temporary, but I have been dealing with this shit for almost five years.

People are always telling me how smart and talented I am, but they don't realize that doesn't mean anything in the world I live in, where the people *seem* smarter or more talented.

People always tell me to be strong and patient and wait, as if I haven't been the one to work twelve hour days in a dive restaurant to make ends meet, or work two jobs and not sleep. I am strong. Strong doesn't pay bills or soothe hurting hearts.

People think my problems aren't big because I have a girlfriend. *Newsflash*…having a girlfriend makes it harder because I don't want the people I love to suffer because of me.

And then there's…

other stuff

My family lives too far away.
They are in bad relationships and don't care.
They are depressed and don't know it.
Black women make me angry.

All the shit on TV is trash.

People are so mean and fake to each other.

I don't feel as close to some people as they feel to me.

I miss my college sisters so much.
My closest friends live too far away.
They all make more money than me.

I want to be better for them.

I want to be the person they all think and say I am.

I don't want to disappoint my girlfriend, family, or friends.

I am scared that I will…

But what makes me maddest is the….

I know better stuff…

It's hard to be authentic, honest, and strong all the time.

I am always in a state of panic and anxiety. I don't have any
insurance to help with the panic and anxiety.

I don't have any insurance because I keep working part time
jobs or serving jobs to make ends meet. In the end, it doesn't

do anything but put me further behind my peers and in more f***ing debt!

I know that "it is what it is" and I am the only person that can change any of this, but that just makes shit more stressful.

Plus, I am tired of trying so hard.

I have a million great ideas and no capital to make them work.

I am mentally and emotionally exhausted.

I don't have all the answers.
I wish I had all the answers.
I feel like I should have more of the answers.

I know my attitude and anger are not helping, but I don't know what to do about the anger and the anxiety.

I know I can't quit or stop or shut down…but some days I want to.

I feel ungrateful when I complain.
I feel inauthentic when I am not honest about how I feel.
I know I am too hard on myself.

I expect better...even though I know I am doing my best.

It's not that I am lazy…I'm just tired.

I'm frustrated. Hurt. Mad. Scared. Annoyed. Just pissed the f*** off.

Whew. Ok. Now back to pretending like everything is fine.

reflections on the true nature of human beings

"You Are Not a Wolf"
April 17, 2012 @ 10:53 AM

I am sure that many of you are familiar with the popular children's story *The Jungle Book*. It's about a boy who was raised by wolves. The story says the boy, Mowgli, was abandoned in the woods and was taken in by a pack of wolves. The wolves discovered him and reared him as their own. Surrounded by wolves and other creatures of the jungle, over time Mowgli began to think he was a wolf.

This story came to my mind a few days ago after I had the unique pleasure of hearing my metaphysical crush, Dr. Deepak Chopra, speak at Georgia State University. Dr. Chopra's two hour lecture ran the gamut of biological and New Thought topics. He explained that human beings are composed of literal stardust and told us that we share 70 percent of our DNA with mosquitoes. He's brilliant in the way he effortlessly fuses quantum physics, metaphysics, astronomy, biology, nutrition, and spirituality with tact and precision. He made a myriad of points that were worth noting, two of which I wanted to share with you today.

The first point he made detailed the spiritual difference between human beings and animals. Dr. Chopra explained that the anatomy of the human brain has evolved over time.

Back when we were cavemen, our brains were much simpler. In function, they closely mirrored that of an animal. He said that, in those days, we devoted the majority of our mental activity to surviving...hunting, gathering, and reproducing. Over the years, our brains have become more multifarious and now include the ability to solve complex problems. So, even though human beings share 98.5 percent of our DNA with chimpanzees, that last little 1.5 percent contains something special.

Human beings are the only form of life to be given the power of discernment. Meaning, we not only have the ability to think, but to create by way of focused attention (or intention). This is important because other living beings do not have this ability. Animals, even the more intelligent species like chimps, exist in a world of duty and necessity. They do what they have to do to survive. There is very little real choice involved. What is more, they are not mentally or emotionally capable of using their minds to create their realities. This is something that only humans can do. Now, let's keep this little tidbit in our back pocket for now, because it's the next point that caused me to have an "ah-ha" moment, of my own.

The second point he made was about the universal connectivity of all living beings. He said that with each breath we literally inhale and exhale cells from every part of our body. Simultaneously, other people are doing the same. So in essence, the simple act of breathing is really a mental and physical exchange of ideas and life.

179

Knowing this makes it easier to understand the Law of Attraction. Think about it, if we are literally sharing our minds with each other, it makes sense that what we focus on manifests. When we are devoting the power of our brain to something, the people around us are responding to our thoughts because—through breath—our thoughts and feelings are becoming a part of them.

Bringing it back to the Jungle Book example, part of the reason Mowgli was unable to see himself as human was because he was surrounded by wolves. Meaning that, he was sharing his thoughts with other wolves. So, in spite of all the physical and emotional evidence that he was human, he still accepted and believed he was a wolf. Mowgli's beliefs are central here because I have no doubt that he intellectually understood that he was not wolf…but his history and surroundings made it hard for him to let his behavior reflect that knowledge.

Now that we know that we share our minds with every person whose air we share, it's easier to see how much our individual consciousness relates to the collective consciousness. We are not *just* what we think about…we are also *who* we think about it with. The danger here is that everyone is not aware of their power as human beings.

Many people move through their lives in survival mode, using only the prehistoric part of their brains that I spoke about earlier. They don't accept the power that they have as humans even though they logically understand it. The problem is, when one person is unwilling to accept who they are, we all suffer.

Think about it:

- You think you are poor because the people around you constantly speak of lack.

- You think you are ugly because you don't match the world's standard of beauty.

- You think you won't find love because your parents were never married and your friends are in bad relationships.

- You think you can't lose weight because we live in culture where dieting has become more popular than healthy living.

- You think you are powerless over your situation because your parents, religion, and culture has taught you that you have no control over what happens to you.

There are millions of other examples I could site, but you get my point. The paradigm shift required to move from being a nation of passive followers to being a nation of enlightened creators, lies in our ability to accept our true nature as humans.

We are creators. Our minds have evolved beyond an existence of survival to an existence of conception. So what we intend, we have the power to conceive. Everything that exists in the physical world came from an idea. The computer you are reading this on, the chair you are sitting in, the clothes you are wearing—were all ideas first. No wolf can boast to that type of achievement. Why then do we lower ourselves to the level of animals by resigning ourselves to survive instead of live? And by live, I mean create and bring joy to others.

As a human, there is power in your thoughts and intentions. And each thought you have has the power to impact every other person you come into contact with. Others may not know or accept it, but if each of us makes a small change each day, we can literally change the world.

I understand that we think we are wolves because we are surrounded by people who think they are wolves. But the truth is, no matter what your history has been, who raised you, or how the people around you behave, remember...

You are not a wolf. You are a human (Now, act like it).

"Divine Intervention"
October 1, 2011 @ 9:47 AM

So, I am putting the final touches on my proposal, when my half-wife[28] calls me and tells me to stop so she can make some edits. I'm paralyzed. I know she needs to help me, but I'm too nervous and edgy to let her. I haven't slept or really

---

[28] Half-wife is a pet name I use to refer to my girlfriend. We are not married and not formally engaged. However we have exchanged rings and plan to marry in the near future.

eaten since Thursday night and, I am having a hard time relinquishing control. I figure I have some time on my hands and I am a little anxious, so I decide to do what I always do when I'm nervous. Read. I was thumbing through some of my old journals and blogs, when I found this. You will be surprised how appropriate it is for my current situation. It really made me feel better. And anything that makes me feels good...I simply must share with my "Fireworks." (Keep in mind, I wrote what you are about to read two years ago! And I didn't change it at all.) How crazy is it that my two-year-ago self knew exactly what I needed to read today. Enjoy.

(This was originally published on January 31, 2009 @ 5:11 PM)

My best friend never misses an opportunity to remind me that the Universe is much smarter than I will ever be. So when the Universe speaks, it would behoove me to listen. With little or no effort on my part the Universe works to ensure that the situations, people, and experiences that I have are always in the best interest of my growth.

I recognize now, that in the past, I have devoted quite a bit of my energy to trying to understand, or even change undesirable circumstances. I felt that I knew better and was under the illusion that my opposition would somehow change things to be the way I wanted them to be. I learned the hard way that living your life this way will make you unhappy. The unhappiness comes because you are not in alignment with what "is." Instead, you are steeped in what "was" or what "should be." However, one need only observe the natural order of things to realize that opposition only deepens the illusion. Acceptance transmutes it.

Surrender is one of the most liberating experiences one can create. Surrender is beyond deciphering what is "fair" or "right," or what is "just" or "good." It is the S P A C E between peace and enlightenment. It is a deep trust for the natural order of the world, for the "is-ness" of your current situation without judgment. I mean, think about it, if we trust God and nature with sustaining our lives, (via the sun that grows the food we eat, and the air and water that sustain our human form), why do we offer so much resistance when this same energy source does something that we don't like?

I have relinquished the need for understanding and replaced it with the will to trust and the desire to surrender. There is a peace in observing both what the Universe brings into my life and what it takes away. I know that I am not diminished by a pushy supervisor, a bad hair day, a few extra pounds, or even a failed relationship. I offer no opposition. I accept and embrace it all...with gratitude.

I am the S P A C E.

Space

I am

The S P A C E.

I am.

"I was" buried beneath the weight of memories.

"I will be" lost in the conceptual fog of cloudlike dreams.

I am the vigilant observer.

The S P A C E

of **all**…

that **is**

(in)between.

References

Byrne, Rhonda. "The Secret." Prime Time Productions.
Sept. 13, 2007. DVD.

Changing Minds. "Coping Mechanisms" Accessed on
January 4, 2013.
http://changingminds.org/explanations/behaviors/coping
/coping.htm.

Changing Minds. "Schema." Accessed on January 3, 2013.
http://changingminds.org/explanations/theories/schema.
htm

Comer. R.J. *Abnormal Psychology.* 4th ed. New York:
Worth Publishing, 2002.

Festinger, L. *A Theory of Cognitive Dissonance.* Palo Alto,
Calif.: Stanford University Press, 1957.

Heartcompass Enterprises and The Foundation for A Mind
and Heart. "Modern Metaphysics: Exploring the True
Nature of Reality with Science and Technology.
Accessed on January 5, 2013. http://www.metaphysics-
for-life.com/modern-metaphysics.html.

Myers, David G. *Social Psychology.* 7th ed. Columbus,
Ohio: McGraw-Hill Higher Education, 2002.

Sternberg, Robert. *In Search of the Human Mind,* 2nd ed.
San Diego: Harcourt Brace College Publishers, 1998.

The Encyclopedia Britannica Company. "Forsake"
Accessed on August 13, 2012. http://www.merriam-
webster.com/dictionary/forsake.

The Free Dictionary by Farlex. "Affinity." Accessed on
October 11, 2011.
http://www.thefreedictionary.com/affinity.

Tolle, Eckhart. *The Power of Now: A Guide to Spiritual Enlightenment*. Novato, Calif.: New World Library & Namaste Publishing, 2004.

Whitbourne, Susan K. "The Essential Guide to Defense Mechanisms." Psychology Today. (2011) 2. Accessed on January 3, 2013.

Titles of Related Interest

Books

Change Your Thoughts, Change Your Life
By Dr. Wayne Dyer

Stand Up For Your Life
By Cheryl Richardson

The Power of Now
By Dr. Eckhart Tolle

A New Earth
By Dr. Eckhart Tolle

Acts of Faith
By Iyanla Vanzant

Films

The Secret, starring Bob Proctor, Joe Vitale, John Assaraf, and Abraham Hicks.
www.thesecret.tv

You Can Heal Your Life, starring Louise L. Hay & friends.
www.louisehaymovie.com

What The Bleep Down The Rabbit Hole, starring Marlee Matlin, Elaine Hendrix, and Barry Newman
www.whatthebleep.com/rabbithole/

About the Author

Kenya A. Jackson, MS

Kenya Jackson is a writer, motivational speaker, and performance poet. She has performed competitively for more than half her life, and has been featured in a variety of artist showcases throughout Atlanta and her hometown of Cleveland.

Prior to becoming a writer, Kenya attended Xavier University where she received dual undergraduate degrees in Sociology and Psychology. Consequently, she spent the early years of her career working with victims of chronic schizophrenia and other personality disorders.

After college, Kenya received her master's degree in Policy Analysis and Nonprofit Management from Georgia State University. She has worked in the nonprofit field since 2004.

Kenya is also the force behind the *#silenceBEseen* Facebook community; a community that emphasizes the importance of changing the world by changing yourself and leading by example. Her ultimate goal is to marry her love for writing, spirituality, and mental health to help other quarterlifers pursue their passions. Kenya's writing has been called smart, honest, and candid—evoking introspective conversation and countless "ah-ha" moments.

Kenya is active in a variety of "new thought" spiritual organizations, The Spiritual Living Center of Atlanta and the Kadampa Meditation Center of Georgia, specifically. She is the administrator of a new-thought blog, www.silencebeseen.com, and has been a staff writer for theFreshXpress.com, and B.O.S.S. e-magazine. Kenya is recently engaged to her partner of three years, Michelle.

more?

Web and book sales: www.kenyajackson.com
Blog: www.silencebeseen.com
Facebook: www.facebook.com/myquarterlife
Twitter: https://twitter.com/silenceBEseen
Instagram: http://instagram.com/silencebeseen

Special Thanks

Donors: Your generous financial gifts made it possible for me to jumpstart the publishing process. Thank you for believing in me and supporting me when I needed it the most. I will never forget your kindness.

Jessica Booth, Henry and Danielle Burton, Sebastian and Yvonne Eich, Aaron and Natasha Holiday, Tracey Pickett, Michelle Saulters, and Juan and Kecia Stewart

Pre-readers/Reviewers: Thank you for providing your time and insight in the developing stages of this work. Your feedback helped shape the content and character of this book.

Tabitha Brown, Chancey Beaty, Neisha Cameron, Qiana Cutts, Sojourner Grimmett, Nik Nicholson Kimberly Offord, and Ann Thomas

Supporters: Thank you for being among the first to purchase my book. I pray you enjoy reading it as much as I enjoyed writing it.

Shemariah Arki, Ryann Bradford, June Brown, M. Tamara Brummer, Danielle Moore-Burton, Kattina Byse, Ricjunette Addie-Carson, Casey Ellerby, Ashley Evans, Jasmine Forts, Lakara Foster, Gloria Freelon, Jessica Greathouse, Angela

Harris, Tara Harris, Tamekia Johnson, Brandy Kellom, Kourtney Kelley, Toya Knox, Crystal Pinkney, Bianca Rodriguez, Tiffany Rowe, Angela Sehzue, Temilola Sobomehin, Antionette Tompkins, Crystal Williams, and Bijoux Wright

Also, to anyone who offered a kind word or any encouragement along the way. Thank you for helping to make my dream a reality.